T0401247

TRUST, TRUSTWORTHINESS, AND STEWARDSHIP

A TRANSFORMATIVE APPROACH

BUSINESS ISSUES, COMPETITION AND ENTREPRENEURSHIP

Additional books and e-books in this series can be found on Nova's website under the Series tab.

TRUST, TRUSTWORTHINESS, AND STEWARDSHIP

A TRANSFORMATIVE APPROACH

CAM CALDWELL, PHD

AND

VERL ANDERSON, PHD

nova
science publishers
New York

NOTICE TO THE READER

Library of Congress Cataloging-in-Publication Data

ISBN: 978-1-53615-093-3

Published by Nova Science Publishers, Inc. † New York

CONTENTS

PREFACE

This new book identifies insights about the ethical issues associated with trust and trustworthiness, and their relationship to the leader's obligations as an ethical steward. The purpose of this book is to identify the importance of trust and trustworthiness in the "Transformative Era," a time when constant change and the increasing demands of customers make it paramount for organizations to obtain the commitment, followership, and extra-role behaviors required to compete in a volatile, uncertain, complex, and ambiguous global marketplace. Unfortunately, leaders today have failed to earn the trust of others by creating arms-length transactional relationships that destroy employee commitment. This book frames the characteristics of the "Transformative Era" and explains how leaders can restore the trust that they have lost by honoring the steward's obligation to create long-term wealth and serve the interests of all stakeholders.

In a world where 71% of all employees are actively looking for new job opportunities and only 16% of employees worldwide describe themselves as "actively engaged" in their work, the importance of reframing the employer-employee relationship demands immediate attention. This book identifies the conditions which make up today's "Transformative Era" and explains how and why leaders destroy trust in the modern organization. It then identifies how leaders can adopt a Transformative Approach to creating organizations that are prepared to survive the turmoil of the modern economy.

Chapter 1

INTRODUCTION AND OVERVIEW: TRUST, TRUSTWORTHINESS, AND STEWARDSHIP

To trust someone is to bestow upon them a great honor and includes the acknowledgement that the person trusted is worthy of one's individual commitment. When trust is complete and deeply committed, trust rivals love in its power to make a difference in relationships and in organizations. In truth, trust encompasses and is motivated by deep respect, and it is often acknowledged that "To be respected is greater than to be loved."

When trust is complete and deeply committed, trust rivals love in its power to make a difference in relationships and in organizations. In truth, trust encompasses and is motivated by deep respect, and it is often acknowledged that "To be respected is greater than to be loved."

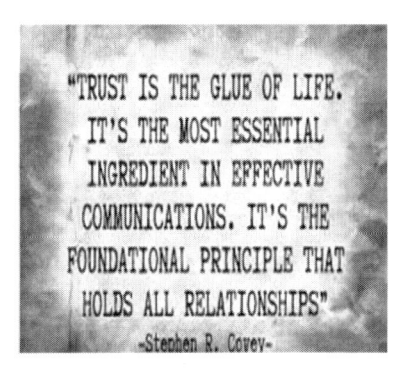

"TRUST IS THE GLUE OF LIFE. IT'S THE MOST ESSENTIAL INGREDIENT IN EFFECTIVE COMMUNICATIONS. IT'S THE FOUNDATIONAL PRINCIPLE THAT HOLDS ALL RELATIONSHIPS"
-Stephen R. Covey-

The focus of this book is on the importance of trust and its antecedent, trustworthiness, in creating the dedication, commitment, and followership of others . . . and the role of stewardship as a transformative approach to leadership that is a foundation for great trust. We begin this book by briefly introducing the three important concepts upon which this book is based. By providing in this chapter a brief description of trust, trustworthiness, and stewardship we lay the foundation for the ten chapters that follow and provide the reader with a succinct summary of the contents that follows.

This chapter begins by defining trust as an interpersonal and organizational construct that has been repeatedly described as the foundation of human relationships and interactions. We then identify the importance of trustworthiness and the qualities upon which it is based in affecting each individual's decision to trust. We then provide a basic description of stewardship as a special type of leadership and governance that merits special attention in the difficult context of the 21st century.

After that relatively brief introduction, we describe the contents of the ten additional chapters that follow, identifying for each reader a summary of the chapters' contents so that readers may have the option to select the chapters of greatest interest to them in the order in which they choose to read about each topic. This chapter concludes with brief comments from the authors about the potential importance of readers becoming highly trusted ethical stewards.

INTRODUCING TRUST

The definition of trust has been a source of controversy for decades[1] . .. but it is universally agreed that trust reinforces and cements relationships when it is present and undermines the effectiveness of individuals and

---

[1] Literally tens of thousands of books and more than one million articles have been written about trust. For a brief summary of the confusion about trust, see, for example, Hosmer, L. T., (1995). "Trust: The Connecting Link between Organizational Theory and Philosophical Ethics." *Academy of Management Review*, Vol. 20, Iss. 2, pp. 379-403.

organizations when it is low[2]. Trust at its optimum creates a mutuality of commitment based upon a shared understanding of duties and obligations that transcend a transactional exchange to include a genuine caring for the best interests of the other party. Trust is based upon an assurance that one is in tune with, in harmony with, and resonating with another party in pursuit of shared interests.

Trust at its optimum creates a mutuality of commitment based upon a shared understanding of duties and obligations that transcend a transactional exchange to include a genuine caring for the best interests of the other party. Trust is based upon an assurance that one is in tune with, in harmony with, and resonating with another party in pursuit of shared interests.

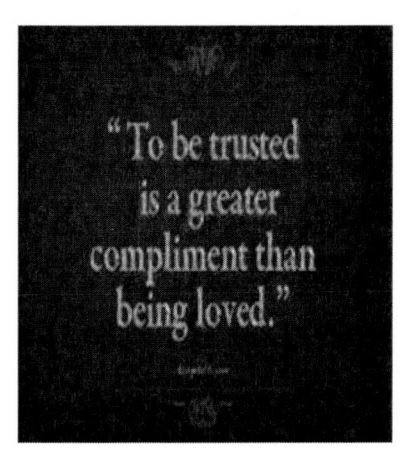

"To be trusted is a greater compliment than being loved."

At its highest level, trust transcends mere cognitive assessment and intent and encompasses an emotional connection that binds the parties, removes doubts and uncertainty about others' intentions, and frees the trusting party to act without restraint or the holding back of commitment or effort. Trust is based upon an assurance that one is in tune with, in harmony with, and resonating with another party in pursuit of shared interests[3]. At its optimum, the trust decision affirms, "I know you, I understand you, I believe in you, I honor you by creating this mutual relationship, and without conditions I empower you by giving of myself on your behalf." That level of trust is unusual and perhaps even rare. It withholds no reservations and

---

[2] A classic and frequently-cited article about the nature of trust is Mayer, R. C., Davis, J. H. & Schoorman, F., (1995). "An Integrative Model of Organizational Trust." *Academy of Management Review*, Vol. 20, Iss. 3, pp. 709-734.

[3] For a review of the intensely personal nature of trust, see Caldwell, C. (2018). *Leadership, Ethics, and Trust*. Newcastle upon Tyne, UK: Cambridge Scholars Publishing.

willingly and passionately persists in its efforts. Trust is the willing and complete opening of the mind and the heart to another[4].

At its optimum, the trust decision affirms, "I know you, I understand you, I believe in you, I honor you by creating this mutual relationship, and without conditions I empower you by giving of myself on your behalf."

The Importance of Trustworthiness

Each individual trusts another person when the trustor perceives that the other person or party is worthy of that trust[5]. The decision made is entirely personal and is based upon the unique values, beliefs, and perceptions of the trustor[6]. In every case, the behaviors, reputation, and communications of the party to be trusted are evaluated by the trusting party who makes an assessment as to the likelihood that the other person or party will honor what are perceived to be duties owed. The willingness to risk or propensity to trust is also based upon the subjective experiences of the trusting party[7].

---

[4] *Ibid.*

[5] This point about being worthy is the point of Caldwell, C., and Ndalamba, K. K., 2017. "Trust and Being 'Worthy' – The Keys to Creating Wealth." *Journal of Management Development*, Vol. 36, Iss. 8, pp. 1076-1086.

[6] See Mayer, R. C., Davis, J. H. & Schoorman, F., (1995), *op. cit.* This key point is also the message of Caldwell, C. and Clapham, S., (2003). "Organizational Trustworthiness: An International Perspective." *Journal of Business Ethics*, Part 1, Vol. 47, Iss. 4, pp. 349-364 and the subject of Caldwell, C., (2004). *Organizational Trustworthiness: A Developmental Model*. Pullman, WA: Washington State University Press.

[7] *Ibid.*

The nature of trustworthiness, although dependent upon perceptions about another party's actions and reputation, is also a product of the life experiences of the person making the decision to trust – and that decision to trust is not usually made lightly

The nature of trustworthiness, although dependent upon perceptions about another party's actions and reputation, is also a product of the life experiences of the person making the decision to trust – and that decision to trust is not usually made lightly. Perceived trustworthiness may take repeated efforts and a considerable amount of time to earn, yet it may be destroyed instantly – even when the trustor has little more than a subjective perception about the party being trusted[8]. Without establishing a reputation as being trustworthy, leaders and organizations are likely to be viewed with reserve, doubt, and skepticism.

To be perceived as fully trustworthy, an individual or party is acknowledged to be the possessor of esteemed qualities that merit high regard and personal commitment.

Trust

Trustworthiness

---

[8] *Ibid.*

To be perceived as fully trustworthy, an individual or party is acknowledged to be the possessor of esteemed qualities that merit high regard and personal commitment. In building relationships, the party seeking to be trusted enhances a reputation for trustworthiness by seeking to understand the criteria by which the trustor willingly trusts and by then meeting the requirements of that trustor's standards. Understanding the individual with whom a leader or organization seeks to establish a high trust relationship is a critical step in earning the trust of the trustor[9].

Stewardship as Enlightened Leadership

Stewardship transcends traditional leadership. The ethical steward seeks outcomes that are virtuous and flourishing – honoring what are often perceived as "covenantal" obligations and responsibilities owed to others[10]. Stewardship is rooted in a philosophy of governance based upon assumptions about the sacred nature of relationships with others[11]. By honoring others, stewards demonstrate their worthiness to be trusted[12]. Ethical stewards focus on creating value for the larger community and view their role as demonstrating a commitment to the pursuit of long-term value creation[13]. As stewards who owe duties to all stakeholders, the steward seeks to optimize the creation of wealth while also acknowledging the obligations and responsibilities due to society – including stakeholders of future generations[14].

---

[9] *Ibid.*

[10] See Cameron, K., (2011). "Responsible Leadership as Virtuous Leadership." Journal of Business Ethics, Vol. 98, pp. 25-35, Caldwell, C., Hayes, L., & Long, D., (2010). "Leadership, Trustworthiness, and Ethical Stewardship." *Journal of Business Ethics*, Vol. 96, Iss. 4, pp. 497-512, and Caldwell, C., Hayes, L., Karri, R., & Bernal, P., (2008). "Ethical Stewardship: The Role of Leadership Behavior and Perceived Trustworthiness." *Journal of Business Ethics*, Vol. 78, Iss. 1/2, pp. 153-164.

[11] Hernandez, M., (2012). "Toward an Understanding of the Psychology of Stewardship." *Academy of Management Review*, Vol. 37, Iss. 2, pp. 172-193.

[12] *Ibid.*

[13] See Caldwell, C., Karri, R., & Vollmar, P., (2006). "Principal Theory and Principle Theory: Ethical Governance from the Follower's Perspective." *Journal of Business Ethics*, Vol. 66, Iss. 2-3, pp. 207-223.

[14] *Ibid.*

> The ethical steward seeks outcomes that are virtuous and flourishing – honoring what are often perceived as "covenantal" obligations and responsibilities owed to others.

The logic of the relationship between trust, trustworthiness, and stewardship is linear and straight forward. An individual who honors the standards of an ethical steward is exponentially more likely than others who lack those standards to be perceived as trustworthy – leading to the trust behavior of the trustor[15]. As leaders strive to become ethical stewards, they enhance their ability to be perceived as trustworthy and to merit the trust and followership of others[16]. By earning that trust, they serve others' interests while also optimizing the likelihood of creating long-term wealth and value[17].

> The logic of the relationship between trust, trustworthiness, and stewardship is linear and straight forward. An individual who honors the standards of an ethical steward is exponentially more likely than others who lack those standards to be perceived as trustworthy – leading to the trust behavior of the trustor.

---

[15] Caldwell, C., Hayes, L. & Long, D., (2010), *op. cit.*
[16] *Ibid.*
[17] Caldwell, C., & Hansen, M., (2010). "Trustworthiness, Governance, and Wealth Creation." *Journal of Business Ethics*, Vol. 97, Iss. 2, pp. 173-188.

Integrating the Concepts

The goal of this book is to provide readers with insights about the nature of the three concepts of trust, trustworthiness, and stewardship. By clarifying that relationship and by identifying how leaders can earn the status of ethical stewards, the chapters that follow provide readers with the ability to transform their philosophy of leadership and governance and to merit being thought of by others as stewards.

This book serves as a resource for self-assessment and increased understanding as would-be leaders strive to increase their awareness of their own highest potential. Stewardship demands a moral and ethical sensitivity to the needs of others and the ability to respond to those needs with the authentic caring demonstrated by the best of leaders. Becoming an ethical steward requires individuals to understand the heart of leadership, as well as the importance of the skills and knowledge that competent leadership demands.

SUMMARY OF THE CHAPTERS

Each of the remaining chapters of this book is now summarized to provide readers with the information about their content. Although the chapters are presented in a logical series to facilitate incremental understanding of the book's contents, readers may benefit by these summaries in seeking to obtain information about a specific topic covered herein.

Chapter Two: The Need for Better Leaders – A Predictable Problem

The purposes of this chapter are to identify twelve barriers that leaders have struggled to overcome and to explain why these obstacles make being a leader so difficult. The chapter begins by proposing a tongue-in-cheek definition of the leader's challenge in today's cynical world – putting into context the extremely complex task that leaders often face. We then identify twelve frequently-recognized barriers that leaders struggle to overcome and comment briefly on why those barriers are daunting for today's leaders. We conclude the chapter with words of encouragement and hope for would-be leaders, suggesting six ideas that others can ponder as they contemplate how they can be perceived as worthy of others' trust.

Chapter Three: Trust from a Transformative Perspective

This chapter provides a transformative perspective of trust – focused on the importance of ethical and practical insights about the nature of trust from the perspective of the Theory of Reasoned Action (TRA) and the Six Beliefs Model (SBM) – to present a definition of trust that clarifies its meaning. These two frameworks clarify why the nature of trust is 1) extremely complex, 2) critical to the process of managing change, and 3) absolutely essential in obtaining cooperation and commitment in the modern organization.

Chapter Four: Trustworthiness and Transformative Change

The purpose of this chapter is to identify the nature of trustworthiness as that vital concept equates to both individuals and organizations and to identify how both can be perceived as worthy of others' trust. Just as trust in others is a personal commodity measured on a continuum, trustworthiness is subjectively determined and recognized as a critical element in influencing others and to positively influence their willingness to go the extra mile to follow a leader, to cooperate in a team, or to serve their organization. The chapter begins by summarizing key insights from the management literature about the qualities that contribute to trustworthiness – listing twelve different qualities associated with trustworthiness for leaders and organizations. The chapter then relates those qualities to the process of obtaining the commitment and followership of others in today's fast-changing world. We conclude the chapter by offering eight important insights for helping organizations and their leaders to be perceived as trustworthy.

Chapter Five: Stewardship as a Transformative Model

The purposes of this chapter are 1) to explain the role of stewardship as a philosophy of organizational governance, comparing and contrasting stewardship philosophy with four other governance models with their underlying values and assumptions, and 2) to offer insights as to why a stewardship approach to governance is superior in creating follower trust, achieving desired outcomes, motivating individuals, and creating long-term value for organizations and for society. We begin by clarifying the role and purpose of organization governance in competing successfully in the modern era. We then identify five established models of organization governance and explain why an ethical stewardship philosophy has six important practical advantages when compared to four other governance approaches. We conclude the chapter by enumerating four important value-based priorities that need to be in place for a stewardship philosophy to be successfully implemented as leaders and organizations seek to increase their ability to create wealth and add value for society.

Chapter Six: Transformative Philosophy and Why It Matters – A New Moral Perspective

The focus of this chapter is to propose that leaders who seek to become more effective at earning the trust and followership of others can achieve that goal by developing a Transformative Philosophy to guide their lives. A Transformative Philosophy is a new concept that incorporates the high standards of ethical leadership and service to others. A Transformative Philosophy enables leaders to honor their obligation 1) to pursue long-term wealth creation, 2) to benefit society, 3) to improve organizations, and 4) to assist colleagues to become the best version of themselves. We begin the chapter by defining what it means to be transformative. We then explain the six key elements of Transformative Philosophy – including in that explanation the contribution of each element to building follower commitment and trust. We then offer seven specific suggestions that can assist individuals to develop a meaningful personal Transformative Philosophy. We conclude the chapter with a challenge to individuals to apply those suggestions in their quest to become more effective leaders.

Chapter Seven: Stewardship as a Moral Virtue

The purposes of this chapter are 1) to explain the importance of the pursuit of the superlative as the fundamental characteristic of ethical stewardship, 2) to explain why leaders who adopt a stewardship model of governance honor the highest standards of ethical leadership, 3) to identify why the stewardship approach to serving individuals and organizations enables leaders to be perceived as morally virtuous. Although the stewardship approach to organization governance has been identified as a positive framework for leadership in the past[18], this chapter identifies in

---

[18] Examples of those who have written about stewardship and its importance include Morela Hernandez and Peter Block. See Hernandez, M., (2008). "Promoting Stewardship Behavior in Organizations." Journal of Business Ethics, Vol. 80, Iss. 1, pp. 121-128, Hernandez, M., (2012). "Toward an Understanding of the Psychology of Stewardship." *Academy of*

greater detail why ethical stewardship inspires greater follower trust, increased employee commitment, and the extra-mile dedication required for firms to be competitive in today's global marketplace. We begin the chapter with a brief review of the nature of stewardship and its underlying commitment to long-term wealth creation. We then identify the nature of both masculine and feminine morality, primarily citing the work of Lawrence Kohlberg[19] and Carol Gilligan[20] who are most frequently identified as responsible for defining those two moral models. After identifying the highest standards of morality emphasized by both models, we clarify how stewardship integrates the best qualities of both masculine and feminine morality while also addressing the extremely high standards of Transformative Ethics. We conclude the chapter by identifying five virtuous qualities of stewardship that demonstrate why leaders who adopt that standard of governance are perceived as morally virtuous.

Chapter Eight: Transformative Leadership: Practical Applications and Implications for Trust

The purposes of this chapter are to both describe this new Transformative Leadership (TL) model and identify its practical advantages in earning the trust and followership of today's employees. The chapter begins with a summary of TL and the six leadership perspectives upon which it is based. Following that explanation, we then identify twelve trust-related qualities of TL that clarify how leaders who adopt that leadership model can increase the commitment of those with whom they work. We conclude the chapter with a brief summary.

Management Review, Vol. 37, Iss. 2, pp. 172-193, and Block, P., (2013). *Stewardship: Choosing Service Over Self-Interest*. San Francisco, CA: Jossey-Bass.

[19] Kohlberg, L., (1981). *The Philosophy of Moral Development: Moral Stages and the Idea of Justice*. New York: Harper & Row.

[20] Gilligan, C., (2016). *In a Different Voice: Psychological Theory and Women's Development*. Boston, MA: Harvard University Press.

Chapter Nine: Self-Assessment and the Stewardship Role: What Leaders Often Lack

The focus of this chapter is on recognizing the importance of self-assessment as a critical determining factor that enables an individual to become a steward rather than simply a leader. The chapter premise is that stewardship's commitment to a higher capacity to serve others is due to that person's understanding of herself or himself by integrating important elements of self-assessment. We begin the chapter by briefly framing the importance of the self-assessment process and explaining the concept of the identity standard as a model for one's identity and personal self-assessment. After describing that model, we then identify ten distinct elements of self-assessment that distinguish the leader from the steward. We conclude this chapter with a challenge to those who seek to become great leaders to adopt this higher level of self-assessment to become stewards in today's challenging world.

Chapter Ten: Stewardship and Personal Learning – Raising the Bar

The focus of this chapter is on the nature of the learning process which leaders incorporate as they develop the skills of ethical stewardship. The chapter begins by describing the process of learning that we all engage in as explained by the Theory of Reasoned Action. After identifying the nature of that universal learning process, we identify and describe in depth the five refined virtues that enable leaders to evolve into ethical stewards. Each of these qualities is explained in terms of its ability to provide a leader with increased understanding of the moral obligations of the ethical steward and the capacity to apply that knowledge. The chapter then identifies the process that leaders can follow to incorporate these five virtues of ethical stewardship into their own leadership relationships.

Chapter Eleven: The Virtuous Reward: Finding Your Voice and the Moral Duty

The purposes of this chapter are to address the importance of "finding your voice" as a virtuous personal achievement and to then honor the moral obligation to discover their own unique significance and potential. The chapter begins with a review of the importance of adding value to society – incorporating both Jim Collins' "Hedgehog Concept" and Covey's insights about finding one's voice. After clarifying why finding our own voice is so critical to being a virtuous leader, we then address why helping others to also achieve their best version of themselves is a moral imperative of leaders as well. We conclude the chapter with brief comments about the importance of leaders becoming not only responsible leaders but also virtuous stewards in their service to others.

The 21st Century is a time of great challenges and demands that leaders become not only role models but a transformative force for improving society.

CONCLUSION

As readers contemplate the value of this book and how they can improve their effectiveness, we suggest that they keep in mind the important roles that leaders play in empowering others, serving customers, and contributing to a better world. The 21st Century is a time of great challenges and demands that leaders become not only role models but a transformative force for improving society. Earning the trust of followers is the key to optimizing the ability of individuals and organizations to add value. That trust is earned when leaders are worthy of that trust. As leaders raise the bar and become ethical stewards, they merit the followership required to solve the vexing problems of today's transformative era.

REFERENCES

Block, P., (2013). *Stewardship: Choosing Service Over Self-Interest*. San Francisco, CA: Jossey-Bass.

Caldwell, C. (2018). *Leadership, Ethics, and Trust*. Newcastle upon Tyne, UK: Cambridge Scholars Publishing.

Caldwell, C., and Ndalamba, K. K., 2017. "Trust and Being 'Worthy' – The Keys to Creating Wealth." *Journal of Management Development*, Vol. 36, Iss. 8, pp. 1076-1086.

Caldwell, C., & Hansen, M., (2010). "Trustworthiness, Governance, and Wealth Creation." *Journal of Business Ethics*, Vol. 97, Iss. 2, pp. 173-188.

Caldwell, C., Hayes, L., Karri, R., & Bernal, P., (2008). "Ethical Stewardship: The Role of Leadership Behavior and Perceived Trustworthiness." *Journal of Business Ethics*, Vol. 78, Iss. 1/2, pp. 153-164.

Caldwell, C., Karri, R., & Vollmar, P., (2006). "Principal Theory and Principle Theory: Ethical Governance from the Follower's Perspective." *Journal of Business Ethics*, Vol. 66, Iss. 2-3, pp. 207-223.

Caldwell, C., (2004). *Organizational Trustworthiness: A Developmental Model*. Pullman, WA: Washington State University Press.

Caldwell, C. and Clapham, S., (2003). "Organizational Trustworthiness: An International Perspective." *Journal of Business Ethics*, Part 1, Vol. 47, Iss. 4, pp.349-364

Cameron, K., (2011). "Responsible Leadership as Virtuous Leadership." Journal of Business Ethics, Vol. 98, pp. 25-35, Caldwell, C., Hayes, L., & Long, D., (2010). "Leadership, Trustworthiness, and Ethical Stewardship." *Journal of Business Ethics*, Vol. 96, Iss. 4, pp. 497-512,

Gilligan, C., (2016). *In a Different Voice: Psychological Theory and Women's Development*. Boston, MA: Harvard University Press.

Hernandez, M., (2012). "Toward an Understanding of the Psychology of Stewardship." *Academy of Management Review*, Vol. 37, Iss. 2, pp. 172-193.

Hosmer, L. T., (1995). "Trust: The Connecting Link between Organizational Theory and Philosophical Ethics." *Academy of Management Review*, Vol. 20, Iss. 2, pp. 379-403.

Hernandez, M., (2008). "Promoting Stewardship Behavior in Organizations." Journal of Business Ethics, Vol. 80, Iss. 1, pp. 121-128, Hernandez, M., (2012). "Toward an Understanding of the Psychology of Stewardship." *Academy of Management Review*, Vol. 37, Iss. 2, pp. 172-193,

Kohlberg, L., (1981). *The Philosophy of Moral Development: Moral Stages and the Idea of Justice*. New York: Harper & Row.

Mayer, R. C., Davis, J. H. & Schoorman, F., (1995). "An Integrative Model of Organizational Trust." *Academy of Management Review*, Vol. 20, Iss. 3, pp. 709-734.

Chapter 2

THE NEED FOR BETTER LEADERS – A PREDICTABLE PROBLEM

The responsibilities of leadership have been difficult to meet and history confirms that even the most highly-regarded leaders have had their critics. Historians widely acknowledge that President Abraham Lincoln was not only brutally ridiculed in the press at the time of his presidency but was considered by many to be incapable of being reelected in 1864[21]. Only Sherman's success in capturing Atlanta restored confidence in Lincoln as a leader and enabled him to beat George McLellan, the Democratic Presidential nominee[22].

Similarly, other often-praised US Presidents are treated kinder in retrospect than they were at the time they served in office. Harry S. Truman was condemned as a waffler who frequently failed to take a strong enough position on political issues[23]. Teddy Roosevelt failed in his bid for reelection in 1912[24]. Current US President, Donald Trump, is viewed by many Americans as a divisive force and a public embarrassment – in addition to

[21] Lincoln's life has been chronicled by many scholars. See, for example, Burlingame, M., (2013). *Abraham Lincoln: A Life*. Baltimore, MY: Johns Hopkins University Press.

[22] *Ibid.*

[23] Dallek, R. & Schlesinger Jr. A. M., (2008). *Harry S. Truman: The American Presidents Series. The 33rd President, 1945-1953*. New York: Times Books.

[24] Pringle, H. F., (2003). *Theodore Roosevelt: A Biography*. Wilmington, MA: Mariner Books.

being called "a constant liar" and "an arrogant egomaniac" -- despite his role in leading an economic recovery that most pundits had predicted would be impossible to achieve[25].

Historians widely acknowledge that President Abraham Lincoln was not only brutally ridiculed in the press at the time of his presidency but was considered by many to be incapable of being reelected in 1864.

"LINCOLN AS A MONKEY, HOLDING A COPY OF THE EMANCIPATION PROCLAMATION." by David Strother, Jan. 14, 1863 *Lincoln was often portrayed in the press as a gorilla, monkey, or baboon.*

Current US President, Donald Trump, is viewed by many Americans as a divisive force and a public embarrassment – in addition to being called "a constant liar" and "an arrogant egomaniac" -- despite his role in leading an economic recovery that most pundits had predicted would be impossible to achieve.

The *Harvard Business Review* has reported that leaders in virtually every type of organization today are held in low regard and trust in leaders and in organizations of all types is at a low point[26]. Although it is easy to complain, "We need better leaders," the challenges facing leaders are not

[25] Black, D., (2018). *Donald J. Trump: A President Like No Other*. Washington, D. C.: Regnery Publishing.

[26] Harrington, M., (2017). "Survey: People's Trust Has Declined in Business, Media, Government, and NGO's". *Harvard Business Review*, January 16, 2017 and found online on November 8, 2018 at https://hbr.org/2017/01/survey-peoples-trust-has-declined-in-business-media-government-and-ngos.

only difficult now but have clearly been difficult for millennia. The purposes of this chapter are to identify twelve barriers that leaders have struggled to overcome and to explain why these obstacles make being a leader so difficult. The chapter begins by proposing a tongue-in-cheek definition of the leader's challenge in today's cynical world – putting into context the extremely complex task that leaders often face. We then identify twelve frequently-recognized barriers that leaders struggle to overcome and comment briefly on why those barriers are daunting for today's leaders. We conclude the chapter with words of encouragement and hope for would-be leaders, suggesting six ideas that others can ponder as they contemplate how they can be perceived as worthy of others' trust.

The *Harvard Business Review* has reported that leaders in virtually every type of organization today are held in low regard and trust in leaders and in organizations of all types is at a low point.

THE CHALLENGE OF LEADERSHIP

It is not easy in today's often demanding climate to lead successfully. When dire circumstances make decision-making more critical and when expectations for positive results are increased, the tasks of leadership become harder to master. In addition, the context of leadership has become more complex and leaders face closer scrutiny. Pulitzer Prize winning author, Thomas L. Friedman, has explained that the challenges of modern leadership have become more difficult than they have ever been[27].

---

[27] Friedman has effectively documented the challenges facing leaders and organizations and the difficulties that must be addressed in two excellent books. See Friedman, T. L. (2007). *The*

Respect for leaders in today's highly cynical world has also plummeted and leaders in virtually every context have struggled for respect[28]. Respect toward leaders has diminished so greatly that in the annual Gallup poll seeking to identify the man and woman that respondents admired most, the leading vote getter in every case has been "no one[29]." That collective response confirms the difficulty that leaders have in earning the trust of the public and in establishing a reputation of personal credibility.

Respect toward leaders has diminished so greatly that in the annual Gallup poll seeking to identify the man and woman that respondents admired most, the leading vote getter in every case has been "no one."

Additional research about leaders and leadership help to clarify why trust in leaders is low. Respondents have overwhelmingly cited integrity and honesty as the most important qualities that they respect in leaders[30], but institutional leaders from churches to government leaders are viewed by large portions of the population as both untrustworthy and dishonest. For example, a 2013 Public Policy Polling study reported in the *Washington Post* revealed that Americans rated elected members of Congress as far lower in trustworthiness than used car salesmen, adding that members of Congress

---

World is Flat 3.0: A Brief History of the Twenty-First Century. New York: Picador Press and Friedman, T. L., (2009). *Hot, Flat, and Crowded 2.0: Why We Need a Green Revolution and How It Can Renew America.* New York: Picador Press.

[28] Harrington, M., (2017), *op. cit.*

[29] Gallup conducts an annual survey of the "most admired" man and woman. This result, favoring "none" or "no one" is documented in "Most Admired Man and Woman." Gallup found online on November 8, 2018 at https://news.gallup.com/poll/1678/most-admired-man-woman.aspx.

[30] This point is made in Kouzes, J. M. & Posner, B. Z., (2011). *Credibility: How Leaders Gain and Lose it, Why People Demand It.* San Francisco, CA: Jossey-Bass.

received an approval rating lower than the approval ratings of both lice and root canals[31].

Americans rated elected members of Congress as lower in trustworthiness than used car salesmen, adding that members of Congress received an approval rating lower than the approval ratings of both lice and root canals

"I prefer a root canal!"

Defining the obstacles facing leaders and resolving those problems can often be discouraging. Although leaders are acknowledged to be necessary and can play important roles in achieving organization successes[32], leadership in today's turbulent times is widely acknowledged to be a frustrating challenge[33]. Experts about organizations remind us that we live and work in a world where good is never good enough and where being simply "good" has been summarily described as "the enemy of great[34]." But great is now both expected and demanded by customers, despite seemingly unending obstacles facing leaders[35].

Thus, the difficulty of being effective as a leader and of earning the trust, respect, and commitment of followers continues today, as it has been for many years, to be an imposing task – and a challenge made even more difficult due to the compression of decision-making into a shorter window

[31] Matthews, D., (2013). "Graph of the Day: Congress is Less Popular than Lice, Colonoscopies, and Nickelback." *Washington Post*, January 10, 2013 found online on November 8, 2018 at https://www.washingtonpost.com/news/wonk/wp/2013/01/10/graph-of-the-day-congress-is-less-popular-than-lice-colonoscopies-and-nickelback/?noredirect=on&utm_term=.65e587f7ca25.

[32] See Burns, J. M., (2010). *Leadership*. New York: Harper Perennial.

[33] See Goodwin D. K., (2018). *Leadership in Turbulent Times*. New York: Simon & Schuster.

[34] This key point about the limit of being good are contained in the first six words of Collins, J., (2001). *Good to Great: Why Some Companies Make the Leap. . . And Others Don't*. New York: HarperCollins.

[35] Kouzes, J. M. & Posner, B. Z., (2011), *op. cit.*

of time, coupled with a host of competitive problems. With tongue only partially in cheek, we offer the following as a problem statement that summarizes the onerous responsibility and challenge facing today's modern leader.

Problem Statement

"How can would-be leaders best overcome the constant criticism and cynicism of envying opponents, the microanalysis of a lurking press, the ineptness of weak colleagues, and their own limitations and imperfections to solve difficult-to-define problems in a world of inevitable chaos, constant change, and conflicting opinions as to what constitutes an acceptable solution?"

Confronted with the difficulties summarized in this problem statement, it is no wonder that so many of today's leaders struggle with the challenges that they face.

TWELVE BARRIERS LEADERS FACE

Past history becomes a barrier to leaders who are expected to solve problems that may have previously been ignored until they became catastrophes demanding emergency attention.

Out of a desire to provide a clearer picture about the barriers and obstacles facing today's leaders, we have developed a list of twelve readily recognized problems which those who wish to lead face in leading. Each of these twelve problem areas can be a stumbling block that makes being a successful leader a task not easily accomplished.

History

Past history becomes a barrier to leaders who are expected to solve problems that may have previously been ignored until they became catastrophes demanding emergency attention – even though preparations by prior leaders for dealing with those problems may have never taken place. Stuck with the "gift" of others' limited vision, naivete, or limited foresight many leaders are held accountable for problems that they inherited but for which they are nonetheless criticized.

Sources of information are imperfect and the validity of responses is often questionable. Incomplete information is a continuing problem and the credibility of information is limited by its age and by intervening events which can impact its validity.

Uncertainty

Despite their access to almost limitless amounts of data and information, the ability to interpret that information continues to be problematic or contradictory. Sources of information are imperfect and the validity of responses is often questionable. Incomplete information is a continuing problem and the credibility of information is limited by its age and by intervening events which can impact its validity[36].

---

[36] Hardin, A., Looney, C. A., & Moody, G. D., (2017). "Assessing the Credibility of Decisional Guidance Delivered by Information Systems." *Journal of Management Information Systems,* Vol. 34, Iss. 4, pp. 1143-1168.

Personal Flaws

Leaders are held accountable and not "allowed" to have personal shortcomings. They are often chastised for being real human beings with idiosyncrasies, foibles, and quirks. If they are civil, they are "too nice." If they possess a dominant physical trait, they are "parodied" and insulted. Heaven help a leader if (s)he misspeaks, trips, or spills the soup at dinner! And the past – oh, the past! If a leader has ever committed an error in his or her his life prior to assuming the leader's mantle, those past errors are also fair game.

Enemies

Whether in business or politics, leaders are subject to criticism from built-in opponents. Unsuccessful competitors, victims of their predecessors, or individuals who they once offended are free to "take their shots" at a new leader – regardless of her or his accomplishments or qualifications.

Complexity

Leaders face mind-numbing problems of profound complexity and uncertain causality. Despite the difficulty of the Gordian knots that they are asked to untie, leaders are assumed to be able to find solutions that have baffled past experts and that no other individuals could expect to address as well. Leaders and organizations must be agile and flexible just to survive and resistance to a change in the status quo is a constant problem that leaders face[37].

---

[37] Denning, S., (2018). "The Challenge of Leadership In the Age of the Agile." *Leader to Leader*, Vol. 2018, Issue 89, pp. 20-25.

Leaders face mind-numbing problems of profound complexity and uncertain causality.

Biases

Leaders, like everyone else, see the world through their own "mediating lens." Their personal experiences, their past, their present, and their dreams for the future impose on leaders a set of personal biases and affect the lens through which they perceive reality. The challenge for leaders is to be able to set aside their biases and to learn to listen to how others perceive that same world.

The challenge for leaders is to be able to set aside their biases and to learn to listen to how others perceive that same world.

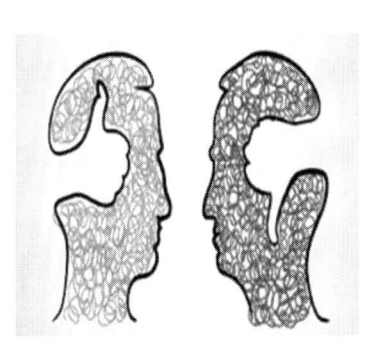

The Press

Reporters from newspapers, television, and the internet make today's leaders the focus of their attention. "Reporting the news" means that an unidentified source could be anyone not named and facts reported in error on Page One today are "corrected" on page sixteen tomorrow. Perish the thought that a news reporter (or his corporate owner) might have a personal agenda or differing point of view!

Social Media

Particularly in the last twenty years, social media have become a daunting obstacle for the modern leader. Anyone and everyone with a Twitter, Facebook, or other social media account can be the critic of a leader . . . and leaders who tweet, twitter, or post may become their own worst enemies. The slightest perceived error can quickly "blow up" the media and become an instant debacle.

Imperfect Resources

Leaders are expected to deal with problems without always having well-qualified staff who may be new to their jobs, inadequately prepared, or even misinformed by their own predecessors. Lack of knowledge about a problem may also be a hindrance to leaders. Despite the limits of their resources and the lack of preparation of those who went before them, leaders are still accountable for all that happens "on their watch," regardless of who actually created the problems.

Egos

Leaders' egos and identities create in them a filter that clouds their judgment and affects their perceptions. Colored by their self-images and their sense of their own self-importance, leaders distort facts, impute negative intentions onto others, and are guilty of self-deception – just like all the rest of us!

> Leaders' egos and identities create in them a filter that clouds their judgment and affects their perceptions

The BIGGER the EGO...

Globalization

The global marketplace has expanded the field of competition, made marketing more complex, and expanded the challenges of decision-making. Globalization also makes it more difficult for companies to attract and retain the best available talent[38].

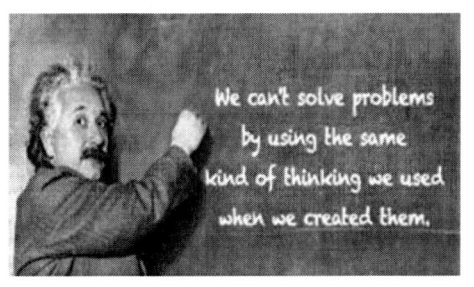

> Leaders act upon their understanding of old problems and old facts . . . but new conditions are constantly arising and old solutions no longer adequately address those new issues.

We can't solve problems by using the same kind of thinking we used when we created them.

Change

We live in a world where conditions constantly change and the ability to address perceived needs is inordinately affected by our "rear view mirror" vision of the world. Leaders act upon their understanding of old problems and old facts . . . but new conditions are constantly arising and old solutions no longer adequately address those new issues.

---

[38] Marschan, A., (2015). "Globalization as a Challenge to Leadership." *FES: Finance, Economy, Strategy.* June 2015, Iss. 5, pp. 9-11.

These twelve problems may not confront every leader in every situation. However, each of these problems – whether singly or in combination with others – can substantially undermine the efforts of an individual or an organization to achieve desired goals. Although these obstacles may not "be a leader's fault," they nevertheless make the leader's task of guiding an organization to success much more imposing.

ENCOURAGING INSIGHTS

The good news for those who would like to become contributing leaders is that there is hope – despite the many difficulties that leaders face. With effort, preparation, and a clear perspective, it is possible for individuals to prepare themselves to be exponentially more effective in overcoming the obstacles that commonly face leaders. However, the evidence also shows that many traditional ideas or "conventional thinking" about leadership must be identified, repudiated, and set aside and replaced with evidence-based true principles[39].

In the chapters that follow in this book, we identify the importance of adopting a "transformative approach" to leadership that incorporates many of the principles of ethical stewardship. As a foreshadowing of those chapters we now suggest six key ideas that can assist individuals to become more effective in dealing with others and in preparing to be leaders.

The evidence shows that many traditional ideas or "conventional thinking" about leadership must be identified, repudiated, and set aside and replaced with evidence-based true principles

---

[39] This crucial point is noted by Pfeffer, J., (1998), *The Human Equation: Building Profits by Putting People First*. Boston, MA: Harvard Business Review Press.

These ideas encompass the concept of a "fundamental state of leadership" advocated by Robert E. Quinn of the University of Michigan and reflect a higher order of excellence to which leaders can strive to attain by becoming the best possible version of themselves[40].

Identify your life's mission and purpose. Write down a statement of who you are and what you wish to achieve in your life.

Be Purpose Driven in Your Approach

Identify your life's mission and purpose. Write down a statement of who you are and what you wish to achieve in your life. Review that statement regularly and use it to guide your actions and the organization in which you work[41].

Move from Being Comfort-Centered to Results-Centered

Be prepared to go outside of your comfort zone and focus on what you need to do to achieve the results that truly matter. Do not be afraid to venture beyond that which is familiar to achieve new and better outcomes[42].

---

[40] See Quinn, R. E., (2005)."Moments of Greatness: Entering the Fundamental State of Leadership." *Harvard Business Review*, July-August, pp. 74-83.

[41] The brilliance of creating a purpose-driven life and a purpose-driven organization are identified in Quinn, R. E. & Thakor, A. V., (2018). "Creating a Purpose-Driven Organization." *Harvard Business Review*, July/August, pp. 78-85.

[42] *Ibid.*

Evolve from Being Externally Directed to Being Internally Directed

Do not base your perceptions about what matters on what others suggest as the applicable standards and values for success. Develop personal integrity and be authentic with regard to the values that you know ought to matter in your life and that sustain your personal character and identity[43]. Recognize the reality that you discover the better you when you benefit the lives of others[44].

Recognize the importance of doing what you do for the purpose of achieving much more than your own self-gratification and self-interest.

Become Less Self-Focused and More Others-Focused

Recognize the importance of doing what you do for the purpose of achieving much more than your own self-gratification and self-interest. Pursuing the collective good creates the trust of others upon which leadership and organizational success are ultimately dependent[45].

Develop the Capacity to be Externally Open

Be open to new opportunities and to the possibilities that present themselves. Divest yourself of defensiveness and resistance to change. Be

---

[43] *Ibid.*

[44] This profound truth is affirmed in Covey, S. R., (2004). *The 8th Habit: From Effectiveness to Greatness*. New York: Free Press.

[45] Quinn, R. E., (2005), *op. cit.*

adaptive and responsive to new images of what is possible. Recognize and embrace the need to constantly adapt to new contexts and needs[46].

Inspire Others to High Performance

Recognize and accept your responsibility to not only to be a role model, a teacher, and a partner with others but become a person who shares power with others, rather than merely exercising power over them. Empower others to become the best that they can be by sharing these ideas with them.

Become a person who shares power with others, rather than merely exercising power over them. Empower others to become the best that they can be by sharing these ideas with them.

Despite the reality that leading others is fraught with difficulty and challenge, the opportunity to lead is also an opportunity to serve and to make a significant difference in the world and in others' lives.

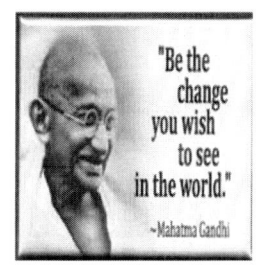

"Be the change you wish to see in the world."
~Mahatma Gandhi

Despite the reality that leading others is fraught with difficulty and challenge, the opportunity to lead is also an opportunity to serve and to make a significant difference in the world and in others' lives. Though the problems that leaders struggle to overcome may be many, the need for better leaders is an absolute prerequisite for achieving noble goals in a world that is constantly struggling.

---

[46] *Ibid.*

Great leaders are desperately needed, and, although they may not always be appreciated, they make a difference in the lives of those with whom they associate and have the potential to also profoundly influence future generations.

As Robert Quinn has noted, leaders can achieve moments of greatness when they prepare themselves to serve others, when they are authentic and purpose driven, and when they are open to opportunities that others may never envision. Great leaders are desperately needed, and, although they may not always be appreciated, they make a difference in the lives of those with whom they associate and have the potential to also profoundly influence future generations. The cost of seeking to become a better person and a more effective leader is not without its risks and its trials . . . but the opportunity to make a difference in the world is worth the effort.

The cost of seeking to become a better person and a more effective leader is not without its risks and its trials . . . but the opportunity to make a difference in the world is worth the effort.

REFERENCES

Black, D., (2018). *Donald J. Trump: A President Like No Other.* Washington, D. C.: Regnery Publishing.

Burlingame, M., (2013). *Abraham Lincoln: A Life.* Baltimore, MY: Johns Hopkins University Press.

Burns, J. M., (2010). *Leadership.* New York: Harper Perennial.

Collins, J., (2001). *Good to Great: Why Some Companies Make the Leap. . . And Others Don't.* New York: HarperCollins.

Covey, S. R., (2004). *The 8ᵗʰ Habit: From Effectiveness to Greatness.* New York: Free Press.

Dallek, R. & Schlesinger Jr. A. M., (2008). *Harry S. Truman: The American Presidents Series. The 33ʳᵈ President, 1945-1953.* New York: Times Books.

Denning, S., (2018). "The Challenge of Leadership In the Age of the Agile." *Leader to Leader,* Vol. 2018, Issue 89, pp. 20-25.

Friedman, T. L. (2007). *The World is Flat 3.0: A Brief History of the Twenty-First Century.* New York: Picador Press and Friedman, T. L., (2009). *Hot, Flat, and Crowded 2.0: Why We Need a Green Revolution and How It Can Renew America.* New York: Picador Press.

Gallup conducts an annual survey of the "most admired" man and woman. This result, favoring "none" or "no one" is documented in *"Most Admired Man and Woman."* Gallup found online on November 8, 2018 at https://news.gallup.com/poll/1678/most-admired-man-woman.aspx.

Goodwin D. K., (2018). *Leadership in Turbulent Times.* New York: Simon & Schuster.

Hardin, A., Looney, C. A., & Moody, G. D., (2017). "Assessing the Credibility of Decisional Guidance Delivered by Information Systems." *Journal of Management Information Systems,* Vol. 34, Iss. 4, pp. 1143-1168.

Harrington, M., (2017). "Survey: People's Trust Has Declined in Business, Media, Government, and NGO's". *Harvard Business Review*, January 16, 2017 and found online on November 8, 2018 at https://hbr.org/2017/01/survey-peoples-trust-has-declined-in-business-media-government-and-ngos.

Kouzes, J. M. & Posner, B. Z., (2011). *Credibility: How Leaders Gain and Lose it, Why People Demand It.* San Francisco, CA: Jossey-Bass.

Marschan, A., (2015). "Globalization as a Challenge to Leadership." *FES: Finance, Economy, Strategy*. June 2015, Iss. 5, pp. 9-11.

Matthews, D., (2013). "Graph of the Day: Congress is Less Popular than Lice, Colonoscopies, and Nickelback." *Washington Post*, January 10, 2013 found online on November 8, 2018 at https://www.washingtonpost.com/news/wonk/wp/2013/01/10/graph-of-the-day-congress-is-less-popular-than-lice-colonoscopies-and-nickelback/?noredirect=on&utm_term=.65e587f7ca25.

Pfeffer, J., (1998), *The Human Equation: Building Profits by Putting People First*. Boston, MA: Harvard Business Review Press.

Pringle, H. F., (2003). *Theodore Roosevelt: A Biography*. Wilmington, MA: Mariner Books.

Quinn, R. E. & Thakor, A. V., (2018). "Creating a Purpose-Driven Organization." *Harvard Business Review*, July/August, pp. 78-85.

Quinn, R. E., (2005)."Moments of Greatness: Entering the Fundamental State of Leadership." *Harvard Business Review*, July-August, pp. 74-83.

Chapter 3

TRUST FROM A TRANSFORMATIVE PERSPECTIVE

The American Supreme Court Justice, Oliver Wendell Holmes is attributed to have written, "I don't give a fig for the simplicity this side of complexity, but I would give my life for the simplicity on the other side of complexity[47]." The skill to reduce complex ideas to insights easily understood is a rare capability – and defining trust is sometimes an effort to get to "the other side of complexity." The definition of trust has often been elusive ground as individuals have struggled to view the actions of others through the lens of their own personal experiences and values. Despite a general consensus that trust is fundamental to cooperation and has been

---

[47] Although the precise wording of this quote has been disputed, there is evidence that Holmes was the source of the idea in a letter to Sir Frederick Pollock. See Howe, M. D., (Ed.) (1961). *Holmes–Pollock Letters: The Correspondence of Mr. Justice Holmes and Sir Frederick Pollock, 1874–1932, Two Volumes in One* (2nd ed.), p. 109 found online on September 1, 2018 at https://en.wikiquote.org/wiki/Oliver_Wendell_Holmes_Jr.

called the glue that holds organizations together[48], trust in leaders and organizations has dropped precipitously[49].

Although millions of articles[50] and more than 50,000 books[51] have been written about trust, the concept remains muddled, its exact nature has been the source of disagreement for decades, and a review of the many definitions of trust suggest that "the far side of complexity" remains uncertain. The purpose of this chapter is to provide a transformative perspective of trust – focused on the importance of ethical and practical insights about the nature of trust from the perspective of the Theory of Reasoned Action (TRA) and the Six Beliefs Model (SBM) – to present a definition of trust that clarifies its meaning. These two frameworks will help to clarify why the nature of trust is 1) extremely complex, 2) critical to the process of managing change, and 3) absolutely essential in obtaining cooperation and commitment in the modern organization.

Decline in Trust

Despite a general consensus that trust is fundamental to cooperation and has been called the glue that holds organizations together, trust in leaders and organizations has dropped precipitously.

---

[48] More than 100 sources have been cited that describe trust as organizational and relational glue. See http://web.a.ebscohost.com/ehost/resultsadvanced?vid=4&sid=7c733d87-fee4-40c8-8b06-60842c651860%40sessionmgr4008&bquery=(TI+Trust)+AND+(TX+glue)&bdata=JmRiPWJ0aCZ0eXBlPTEmc2l0ZT1laG9zdC1saXZl found on September 1, 2018 and Covey, S. R., (2004). *The 8th Habit: From Effectiveness to Greatness*. New York: Free Press and Brainy Quotes, "Stephen Covey Quotes" found online on September 1, 2018 at https://www.brainyquote.com/quotes/stephen_covey_450798.

[49] This startling reality is identified in the 2017 Edelman Trust Barometer found online on September 17, 2018 at https://www.edelman.com/trust2017/,

[50] See Business Source Complete found on September 1, 2018 at http://web.b.ebscohost.com/ehost/resultsadvanced?vid=4&sid=8b312cb3-1cc9-4042-b267-42096174f427%40sessionmgr102&bquery=TX+Trust&bdata=JmRiPWJ0aCZ0eXBlPTEmc2l0ZT1laG9zdC1saXZl.

[51] Confirmed in Amazon.com books found on September 1, 2018 at https://www.amazon.com/s/ref=nb_sb_noss_1?url=search-alias%3Dstripbooks&field-keywords=trust.

The chapter begins with a brief summary of the many facets of trust as an interpersonal construct, using TRA as a framework for explaining why the definitions of trust have been so varied. Using the SBM as a window to understanding each person's unique belief structure, the chapter then clarifies how individuals view the trust relationship and the duties which they perceive that they are owed. Integrating the two frameworks, the chapter summarizes the nature of trust – emphasizing why trust is ultimately best understood as the behavioral response of the person who trusts, based upon his or her perceptions about another party. The chapter concludes with eight suggestions for individuals and organizations interested in creating high trust with others.

TRUST AND THE THEORY OF REASONED ACTION

Theory of Reasoned Action

Cognitive beliefs and affective feelings are integrated into intentions that form the basis for human actions – conditional upon each individual's character, passion, commitment, and an array of external environmental conditions which constantly affect human choices

TRA explains that decision-making associated with human behavior meshes cognitive and emotional perceptions into an assessment of alternatives in responding to the context of a situation and the actions of others. Cognitive beliefs and affective feelings are integrated into intentions that form the basis for human actions – conditional upon each individual's character, passion, commitment, and an array of external environmental conditions which constantly affect human choices[52]. It is the variability of human differences, the non-linearity of decision-making, and the interplay of people and organizations that often makes it difficult to discern how and why people act as they do – or choose not to respond as one might predict and anticipate[53].

Understanding Others

It is the variability of human differences, the non-linearity of decision-making, and the interplay of people and organizations that often makes it difficult to discern how and why people act as they do – or choose not to respond as one might predict and anticipate.

It is not our differences that divide us. It is our inability to recognize, accept, and celebrate those differences.

The complex nature of the basis for individual decisions is a byproduct of the constantly evolving perceptions that each individual has about his or her core beliefs. Those perceptions are based upon cognitive beliefs and affective emotions associated with 1) normative behaviors that guide the self and others, 2) duties owed in relationships, and 3) one's emotional intelligence and abilities in controlling personal responses to others and to the context of situations[54]. Other factors, such as the actions of other persons and external environmental pressures, also influence behavioral choices and a person's confidence. Intentions to act are affected by perceptions about risk, uncertainty, and the likelihood that actions taken w[55]ill achieve a

---

[52] *Ibid.* This succinct summary of how human choices are made integrates the work of Fishbein and Ajzen, as previously cited.

[53] The complexity of human decision-making is well described by Karl Weick in Weick, K. E. (1993). "The Collapse of Sense-Making in Organizations: The Mann Gulch Disaster." *Administrative Science Quarterly*, Vol. 38, Iss. 4, pp. 628-652.

[54] Fishbein, M. & Ajzen, I., (2015), *op. cit.*

[55] *Ibid.*

desired outcome[56]. Diagram 1 is a depiction of the factors determining behaviors associated with the decision to trust in TRA.

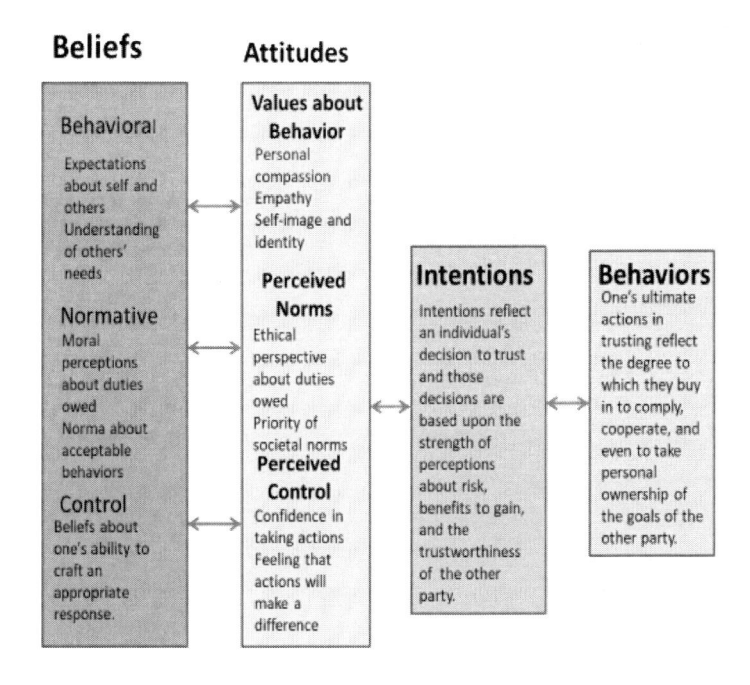

Diagram 1. The Theory of Reasoned Action and Trust Decision-Making.

Beliefs and attitudes constantly interact and create an often-unconscious "conceptual calculus" by which we each make decisions[57]. Those decisions are influenced by a multitude of factors associated with our own identities and self-esteem; our perceptions about the world of the past, present, and future; and the duties we owe to others, to the larger community, and to God[58]. The mediating lens by which we see the world is individual in nature

---

[56] See Vroom, V., (1994). *Work and Motivation*. San Francisco, CA: Jossey-Bass.

[5757] This complex sub-conscious process is described in Creed, W. E. D. & Miles, R. E., (1995). "Trust in Organizations: A Conceptual Framework Linking Organizational Forms, Managerial Philosophies, and the Opportunity Costs of Controls" in *Trust in Organizations: Frontiers of Theory and Research*, Kramer, R. M. & Tyler, T. (Eds.). Thousand Oaks, CA: Sage Publications, pp. 16-38.

[58] These beliefs are described in Caldwell, C., Hayes, L., and Long, D., 2010. "Leadership, Trustworthiness, and Ethical Stewardship." *Journal of Business Ethics*, Vol. 96, Iss. 4, pp. 497-512.

and profoundly complex – constantly affected by our cognitive and affective perceptions about the world in which we live[59]. Our intention to take action that is harmonic and congruent with our beliefs and attitudes is similarly complex with profound identity-based implications about how we view ourselves, the degree to which we have personal integrity, and our capacity for self-deception and denial[60].

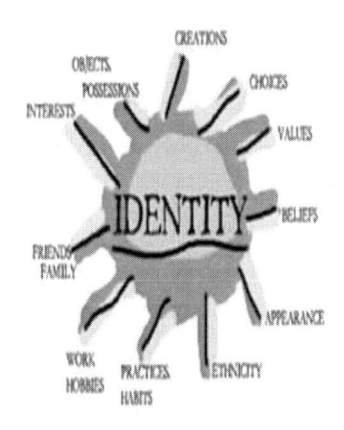

Identity Issues

Our intention to take action that is harmonic and congruent with our beliefs and attitudes is similarly complex with profound identity-based implications about how we view ourselves, the degree to which we have personal integrity, and our capacity for self-deception and denial.

Consistent with the TRA, the decision to trust is also influenced by the beliefs that exist about the psychological contract perceived by the two parties[61]. Psychological contracts are written and unwritten implicit agreements to cooperate between two parties, based upon the assumption that both parties will benefit thereby[62]. As individuals assess their desire to trust others, that trust is influenced by three powerful factors[63]:

---

[59] The profoundly complex nature of our identities and the many internal and external factors that impact our decisions is addressed in many sources. See, for example, Caldwell, C. (2009). "Identity, Self-Deception, and Self-Awareness: Ethical Implications for Leaders and Organizations." *Journal of Business Ethics*, Vol. 90, Supp. 3, pp. 393-406.

[60] *Ibid.*

[61] See Rousseau, D. M., (1995). *Psychological Contracts in Organizations: Understanding Written and Unwritten Agreements*. Thousand Oaks, CA: Sage Publications.

[62] *Ibid.*

[63] The motivation to act is identified as expectancy theory by Vroom. See Vroom, V. H., (1994). *Work and Motivation*. San Francisco, CA: Jossey-Bass.

1. *Whether the cooperative obligations expected of them are within their capacity to perform.* Individuals consciously and unconsciously assess the context of their situations, the resources available to them, their own personal capabilities, and the subjective likelihood that they can reasonably accomplish what they are expected to do;

2. *Whether the other party will honor their commitment to provide a specific benefit.* The other party's likelihood to provide a *quid pro quo* benefit in return for the actions required is assessed, based upon the relationship that exists between the parties and the other party's integrity, ability to provide the desired benefit, and the nature of the relationship between the parties.

3. *Whether the anticipated benefit is deemed significantly important to justify the behavior required.* The benefit is assessed in context with its relative importance and value, depending upon the needs of the party expected to act.

Breach of Trust

This difference in perceptions about obligations owed – whether by themselves or by the other party – can result in the deterioration of trust and the perception that a breach of good faith has occurred. This cause of the destruction of trust in interpersonal and organizational relationships is extremely common.

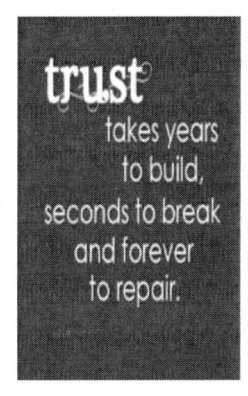

trust takes years to build, seconds to break and forever to repair.

In their respective perceptions of the psychological contract, each party assumes that both parties are committed to mutually understood cooperative action. In fact, however, the two parties involved in working relationships frequently do not understand how their counterpart defines the expectations required of them or owed from them in return[64]. This difference in perceptions about obligations owed – whether by themselves or by the other party – can result in the deterioration of trust and the perception that a breach of good faith has occurred. This cause of the destruction of trust in interpersonal and organizational relationships is extremely common[65]. When perceptions about the nature of the relationship are affected by perceived breaches in the psychological contract between the parties, both the beliefs and attitudes about the other party are seriously impacted and the willingness and intention to trust are seriously affected.

Psychological Contracts

When perceptions about the nature of the relationship are affected by perceived breaches in the psychological contract between the parties, both the beliefs and attitudes about the other party are seriously impacted and the willingness and intention to trust are seriously affected.

Assumptions can kill relationships.

THE SIX BELIEFS MODEL AND TRUST PERCEPTIONS

The SBM is an evolving model developed initially by MIT's Peter Senge to attempt to explain that expectations about future goals positively impact beliefs about one's current reality – although Senge's model was only partially complete[66]. The dynamic tension of an anticipated future motivates

---

[64] The fact that psychological contracts are frequently misunderstood is documented in Robinson, S. L. & Rousseau, D. M., (1994). "Violating the Psychological Contract: Not the Exception but the Norm." *Journal of Organizational Behavior.*, Vol. 15, Iss. 3, pp. 245-259.

[65] *Ibid.*

[66] Senge, P. M., (2006). *The Fifth Discipline: The Art & Practice of the Learning Organization.* New York: Doubleday.

individuals to increase their commitment to improving their status quo or current reality[67]. The SBM is a key element of each individual's mediating lens through which (s)he views the world[68]. Table 1 is a brief summary of each of these six beliefs and their influence on trust perceptions.

These six beliefs influence each individual's priorities, values, and the ethical lens through which each person sees the world. The following is a brief explanation about how these six beliefs influence perceptions about trust and measurably affect trust relationships between individuals and within organizations.

Beliefs about Self

Each individual's identity is profoundly affected by how (s)he views his or her roles in life and the competence in which that person performs those roles. For each person (s)he establishes an identity standard or comparator which serves as a basis for comparing how (s)he "should" behave in interactions with others. That identity standard is sub-consciously constantly compared to one's actual behaviors and serves as a basis for either modifying one's conduct or substantially influencing one's self-image and self-esteem. In large measure, this self-monitoring process takes place without individuals formally assessing their desired behaviors or defining specific standards by which they seek to govern their lives. The impact of beliefs about self-affect how each person presents himself or herself to others and has a profound unconscious impact on how a person interacts. It is not uncommon for individuals to rationalize, justify, and make excuses for their behaviors. It is also typical for people to engage in self-deceptive behaviors and denial of intentions in an effort to preserve their self-esteem. The decision to trust others often unconsciously reflects how one view his or her self.

---

[67] *Ibid.*
[68] See Caldwell, C., and Hayes, L., (2007). "Leadership, Trustworthiness, and the Mediating Lens." *Journal of Management Development.* Vol. 26, Iss. 3, pp. 261-278.

Table 1. Six belief model factors and their relationship to trust

SMB Belief Factors	Description	Impact on Perceptions	Importance to Trust	Comments
Self	Beliefs about one's own identity, values, goals, roles, priorities, and duties owed to others.	Identity standards and self-perceptions affect all interactions with others.	Self-image and self-esteem are trust-related priorities and considered critical in trust decisions.	Self-justification and self-deception influence perceptions of others and willingness to trust.
Others	Significant relationships with others and expectations about roles of and duties owed from others.	Close relationships bias perceptions and influence roles and duties expected.	Relationships are critical to establishing trust or the decision to withhold commitment.	Failure to honor perceived duties owed destroys trust and impairs relationships.
Divine/The World	This consists of beliefs about a divine power or universal duties owed to the community, society, and the world.	Reflects personal expectations about duties owed or about divine obligations.	Assumptions about moral and ethical obligations become the foundation for deciding to trust.	Belief in God not required for a person to accept that (s)he and others are affected by moral obligations.
The Past	Personal and family background and history, significant personal events, roles, relationships, accomplishments, successes and failures.	The past provides the window by which a person looks at the world and greatly influences expectations.	Past experiences greatly influence one's values and expectations about duties owed and how trust is generated & maintained.	The influence of the past typically creates a personal bias and set of expectations about interpersonal interactions.
Current Reality	Perceptions about the present, current roles, present situation, and relationships.	Current needs profoundly influence perceived needs and expectations.	Psychological contracts may vary based upon subjective perceptions about needs.	Trust decisions are influenced in the present according to evolving expectations.
The Future	Goals for the future, hopes and expectations, life plans and desires.	Views about the future are often idealized.	Trust is dependent upon perceptions about support for future goals.	Future desires are related to one's identity and hopes.

Rationalization and Self-Justification

The impact of beliefs about self affect how each person presents himself or herself to others and has a profound unconscious impact on how a person interacts. It is not uncommon for individuals to rationalize, justify, and make excuses for their behaviors.

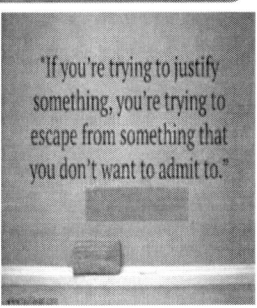

"If you're trying to justify something, you're trying to escape from something that you don't want to admit to."

Beliefs about Others

Expectations about Others

Relationships inevitably include expectations about duties owed to and owed from others and the propensity to trust is affected by personal experiences which a person has had. A common tendency is to project onto other people one's expectations about how one would act in a similar situation.

Others are viewed in many roles and often form the basis for personal comparison. The psychological contracts into which people enter typically involve other individuals with whom a person may interact frequently. Relationships inevitably include expectations about duties owed to and owed from others and the propensity to trust is affected by personal experiences which a person has had. A common tendency is to project onto other people one's expectations about how one would act in a similar situation. It is also common to generalize and to project upon others the experiences that one has had in similar situations in life. Close relationships often significantly alter perceived duties owed to others, as opposed to duties owed to the larger community or to society.

Beliefs about the Divine or the World

One's moral and ethical sense is largely influenced by the role of the divine or the obligations that (s)he believes to be owed to society. The Ethic of Religious Injunction is often accompanied by a specific set of rules outlining obligations to God, to self, and to others. Whether one has a close and personal relationship with God can profoundly influence decisions, self-image, and obligations owed to others. A person may choose to adopt a highly ethical set of personal obligations to society – or may conclude that no such obligations exist. Trust may be viewed as a social, religious, or interpersonal interaction or may be perceived as a calculated decision designed to perpetuate one's self-interests.

Ethical Lens

A person may choose to adopt a highly ethical set of personal obligations to society – or may conclude that no such obligations exist. Trust may be viewed as a social, religious, or interpersonal interaction or may be perceived as a calculated decision designed to perpetuate one's self-interests.

Beliefs about the Past

One's personal history, particularly one's upbringing and family relationships, can have a major impact on one's willingness to trust others.

In addition, significant emotional events which have occurred in one's life can drastically impact an individual's view of the world and the ground rules by which (s)he will relate to others. Social, economic, job-related, religious, and other personal experiences can all play a role in influencing one's view of the world, one's feelings about the predictability of people and settings, and one's willingness to risk.

Significant Emotional Events

Significant emotional events which have occurred in one's life can drastically impact an individual's view of the world and the ground rules by which (s)he will relate to others. Social, economic, job-related, religious, and other personal experiences can all play a role in influencing one's view of the world, one's feelings about the predictability of people and settings, and one's willingness to risk.

Beliefs about Current Reality

Current Reality

The status quo and one's perception of current reality are based upon one's present working conditions, various roles, employment and economic status, physical and emotional health, and relationships with others. Current reality may also be affected by external political and economic factors as well as life-changing and life-influencing events that arise.

Defining reality has been defined as one of the key responsibilities of leadership[69]. The status quo and one's perception of current reality are based upon one's present working conditions, various roles, employment and economic status, physical and emotional health, and relationships with others. Current reality may also be affected by external political and economic factors as well as life-changing and life-influencing events that arise. The degree to which current reality is stable or uncertain directly influences individual perceptions and the willingness to trust.

Beliefs about the Future

Beliefs about the future include personal goals, hopes, and aspirations about life and one's future opportunities. The future is often viewed from a very positive perspective, although one's attitudes can also be influenced by negative current circumstances which suggest unfavorable future consequences. Viewing the future from a positive perspective enhances the willingness to trust while negative projections tend to diminish the willingness to trust.

Future Aspirations

Beliefs about the future include personal goals, hopes, and aspirations about life and one's future opportunities. The future is often viewed from a very positive perspective, although one's attitudes can also be influenced by negative current circumstances which suggest unfavorable future consequences.

---

[69] See DePree, M., (2004). Leadership is an Art. New York: Crown Publishing, p. 11.

One's perceptions based upon the SBM affect the decision to act, the degree of personal commitment encompassed by that action, and the effort made to honor relationships and duties owed to others[70]. In today's highly fluid transformative world, the trust decision depends upon a multitude of very practical factors which influence the nature of each person's subjective response and the degree of their cooperative behavior.

Followers determine their compliance with leaders' requests based upon individual perceptions about the leader's worthiness to lead and the legitimacy of the behavior requested[71]. This insight about the leader-follower relationship confirms that follower trust behaviors are variable and exist on a continuum[72]. The decision to trust is independently made by each person and is carried out as a continuum of personal responses[73]. This continuum ranges from reluctant compliance, often performed only when a supervisor is present and monitoring employee performance, to complete employee commitment wherein the employee acts as a fully-engaged "owner and partner" who acts as a steward of the organization's best interests[74]. Table 2 summarizes the level of individual responses as identified by the compliance-commitment continuum[75].

Integrating insights about trust that are provided by both TRA and the SBM, the nature of trust as a complex and subjectively-perceived concept is more easily understood. Trust has been variously described as a belief, an attitude, an intention, a propensity to act, and as a behavior[76] – and all of

---

[70] Caldwell, C., and Hayes, L., (2007), *op. cit.*

[71] Barnard's lectures to Harvard College were compiled and printed in Barnard, C. I., (1938). *The Functions of the Executive.* Cambridge, MA: Harvard College. That compilation has come to be among the most-cited business texts of all time.

[72] The nature of trust as a response that is manifest on a continuum was addressed in the classic paper Mayer, R. C., Davis, J. H. & Schoorman, F. D. (1995). "An Integrative Model of Organizational Trust." *Academy of Management Review,* Vol. 20, Iss. 3, pp. 709-734.

[73] See Hayes, L., Caldwell, C., Licona, B. and Meyer, T. E., 2015. "Follower Behaviors and Barriers to Wealth Creation." *Journal of Management Development,* Vol. 34, Iss. 3, pp. 270-285.

[74] This compliance-commitment continuum was introduced by Senge, P., (2006), *op. cit.* and is also explained in Caldwell, C. & Hansen, M., (2010). Trustworthiness, Governance, and Wealth Creation." *Journal of Business Ethics,* Vol. 97, Iss. 2, pp. 173-188.

[75] *Ibid.* This table has been only slightly adapted from the original table.

[76] See, for example, Mayer, R. C., Davis, J. H. & Schoorman, F. D. (1995), *op. cit.* and Gullett, J., Canuto-Carranco, M., Brister, M., Turner, S., and Caldwell, C. (2009). "The Buyer-Supplier

those descriptions can be understood in context with TRA. Similarly, the SBM helps to explain why trust is so subjectively perceived and dependent upon many variables that are personal for each individual and that influence his or her values, priorities, and ethical assumptions.

Table 2. Level of trust response and application to trust

Level	Application to trust
Reluctant compliance Does not see the benefit of an expected behavior but complies because of a sense of obligation or duty	Reluctant compliance reflects a conditional willingness to relinquish control, and only to a degree required to avoid the termination of the relationship. Trust is minimal and is combined with distrust with the likely creation of transaction costs associated to ensure compliance.
Formal compliance On the whole sees the general benefits of an expected behavior. Does what is expected but no more	Formal compliance is based upon an express or implied arms-length psychological contract that exists in an exchange relationship that is typically in writing and enforced through transaction costs.
Genuine compliance Recognizes the benefits of an expected behavior. Does what is expected and more. Follows the "letter of the law"	Genuine compliance is present but commitment is intermittent. Level of trust reflects willingness and support, but bounds exist with regard to the degree of personal responsibility included in one's role – with ownership viewed as primarily the responsibility of management.
Enrollment Wants to perform the expected behaviors. Will do whatever can be done within the "spirit of the law." Implies free choice supporting desired goals but at a lower level than full ownership	Enrollment reflects buy-in but below full commitment. Willingness to participate actively is present, but limits exist with regard to the degree of personal ownership. The degree of trust is relatively high with a shared sense of ownership reflecting partial commitment.
Stewardship Commitment Wants to perform the expected behaviors and looks for ways to increase their effectiveness. Will do whatever is necessary to achieve desired outcomes. Not only enrolled but feels fully responsible for desired outcomes	Commitment includes the endorsement of all objectives, extra-role behavior, and extra mile support. Trust is high and ownership of the mission, purpose, and goals of the organization or the purposes of a relationship are fully endorsed.

Relationship: An Integrative Model of Ethics and Trust." *Journal of Business Ethics*, Vol. 90, Supp. 3, pp. 329-341.

Defining Trust

Trust is the relinquishing of one's personal choice to cooperate with another party, in the expectant hope that this other party will honor the duties of the perceived psychological contract between the parties. Measurable on a continuum, trust behavior ranges from compliance to a stewardship commitment which reflects each respondent's degree of trust in the other party.

Combining the diverse perspectives about trust, it is ultimately best identified as a behavior that is subjectively determined by each individual. *Trust is the relinquishing of one's personal choice to cooperate with another party, in the expectant hope that this other party will honor the duties of the perceived psychological contract between the parties. Measurable on a continuum, trust behavior ranges from compliance to a stewardship commitment which reflects each respondent's degree of trust in the other party.* This definition of trust explains the importance of trust whether manifest in a personal relationship with one individual or as a member of a larger organization.

EIGHT SUGGESTIONS FOR INCREASING TRUST

In the transformative era, as individuals and organizations strive to create higher trust with others, there are important principles which can be applied to build trust in relationships and to create aligned and supportive high-trust organization cultures. Building trust demands understanding others at the individual level for trust is an individually-determined subjective perception. The following are eight suggestions for creating and sustaining trust.

1. *Treat all others as valued ends and never as means to your own ends.* The ability to recognize the importance of others is an ethically-based capacity which has been acknowledged to be essential for building relationships[77]. Recognizing the inherent worth of others demonstrates the caring that earns trust and builds shared commitment[78].

The ability to recognize the importance of others is an ethically-based capacity which has been acknowledged to be essential for building relationships.

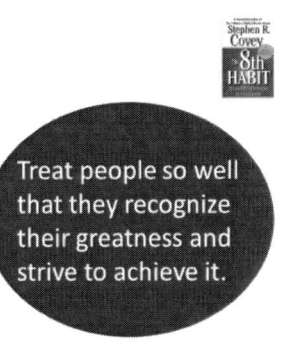

Treat people so well that they recognize their greatness and strive to achieve it.

2. *Be kind and generous in dealing with others.* Building trust by treating others with compassion, kindness, and respect is a leadership approach that is frequently considered to be unique in today's highly competitive world[79]. Focusing on building relationships with others enables leaders to fill the role of being "servants and debtors[80]" – qualities that demonstrate a leader's commitment to others' welfare, growth and wholeness[81].

---

[77] The ethically-based nature of respect for others has been addressed by a number of scholars. See, for example, Gilligan, C., (2016). *In a Different Voice: Psychological Theory and Women's Development*. Boston, MA: Harvard University Press and Anderson, V. & Caldwell, C., (2018). *Humility as Enlightened Leadership*. Hauppage, NY: NOVA Publishing.

[78] This point about treating others in a caring manner is identified in Caldwell, C., Floyd, L. A., Taylor, J and Woodard, B. (2014). "Beneficence as a Source of Competitive Advantage." *Journal of Management Development*, Vol. 33, Iss. 10, pp. 1057-1069.

[79] See Okpala, C. O., Atwijuka, S., & Caldwell, C., (Working Paper). "Compassionate Leadership in an Arms-Length World."

[80] DePree, M., (2004), *op. cit.*

[81] The importance of leaders pursuing the best interests of others is well documented as an important demonstration of effective leadership and the source of trust. See, for example, Caldwell, C., Bischoff, S. J., and Karri, R. (2002). "The Four Umpires: A Paradigm for Ethical Leadership," *Journal of Business Ethics*, Vol. 36, Iss. 1/2, pp. 153-163.

Focusing on building relationships with others enables leaders to fill the role of being "servants and debtors" – qualities that demonstrate a leader's commitment to others' welfare, growth and wholeness.

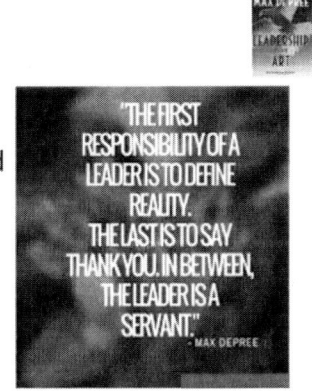

3. *Identify and demonstrate concern for others' expectations.* Understanding the unique nature of the psychological contract enables leaders to be wise in seeking to clarify with others their expectations about duties and obligations owed by both parties[82]. The failure to demonstrate concern for others' perceptions is a lose-lose choice for leaders and exponentially increases the likelihood that trust will be undermined[83].

The failure to demonstrate concern for others' perceptions is a lose-lose choice for leaders and exponentially increases the likelihood that trust will be undermined.

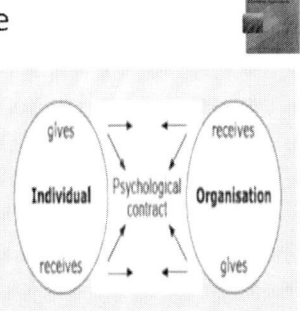

[82] Rousseau, D. M., (1995), *op. cit.*
[83] Robinson, S. L. & Rousseau, D. M., (1994), *op. cit.*

4. *Acknowledge Change as Constant and Embrace It.* Recognizing the realities that face today's transformative world is a necessity for building trust[84]. Although maintaining the status quo is comfortable for others, the reality of today's world is that competition is keener, change is more rapid, and the abilities to adapt and to be flexible are essential for survival[85]. When leaders embrace change and create organization systems that support it, the respect of followers and their willingness to change increases[86].

> Recognizing the realities that face today's transformative world is a necessity for building trust. Although maintaining the status quo is comfortable for others, the reality of today's world is that competition is keener, change is more rapid, and the abilities to adapt and to be flexible are essential for survival.

5. *Help Others to Become their Best.* Leadership is largely about helping others to discover their highest potential and to then assist others to achieve their best[87]. Leadership is largely a covenantal relationship in which leaders owe others the opportunity to excel – and by honoring that sacred responsibility leaders enhance their ability to inspire and motivate others[88].

---

[84] The reality of today's competitive world and the importance of leaders focusing on sharing that reality with others is a clear message in Block, P., (2013). *Stewardship: Choosing Service Over Self-Interest.* San Francisco, CA: Jossey-Bass.

[85] The competitive problems facing business are well documented in Christensen, C. M., (2016). *The Innovator's Dilemma: When New Technologies Cause Great Firms to Fail.* Boston, MA: Harvard Business Review Press.

[86] See Kotter, J. P., (2012). *Leading Change with a New Preface by the Author.* Boston, MA: Harvard Business Review Press.

[87] This message is the theme of Covey, S. R., (2004), *op. cit.* See pp. 98-99 in particular.

[88] See DePree, M., (2004), *op. cit.,* Chapter 1.

Leadership is largely a covenantal relationship in which leaders owe others the opportunity to excel – and by honoring that sacred responsibility leaders enhance their ability to inspire and motivate others.

6. *Find Your Passion and Pursue It.* Leaders earn others' respect and trust and demonstrate their own commitment to excellence when they develop a passion for success and persistently pursue excellence[89]. Passion and perseverance enable leaders to both model the way for others and encourage their hearts[90]. Both key roles build follower trust.

Leaders earn others' respect and trust and demonstrate their own commitment to excellen when they develop a passion for success and persistently pursue excellence.

7. *Seek to Constantly Improve.* Leaders who demonstrate a fierce commitment to constantly improve and to achieve the ultimate best for their organizations are critically important for achieving long-

---

[89] The keys to being effective incorporate both passion and perseverance. Those qualities are well-documented as critical for success by Collins, J., (2001), *op. cit.*, Duckworth, A., (2018). GRIT: *The Power of Passion and Perseverance.* New York: Scribners, and Hansen, M. T., (2018). *Great at Work: How Top Performers Do Less, Work Better, and Achieve More.* New York: Simon & Schuster.

[90] Kouzes, J. M. & Posner, B. Z., (2017). *The Leadership Challenge: How to Make Extraordinary Things Happen in Organizations.* San Francisco, CA: Jossey-Bass.

term organization success and for modeling the virtues of greatness[91]. Those leaders earn personal credibility and the trust of others by their personal integrity, their competence, and their commitment to everyone's success[92].

Leaders earn personal credibility and the trust of others by their personal integrity, their competence, and their commitment to everyone's success.

8. *Honor Commitments and Keep Promises.* By keeping their word, leaders demonstrate that they can be counted on. If, for unexpected reasons, a leader finds herself or himself in a position where (s)he cannot honor a commitment, the leader has an absolute obligation to 1) notify others affected by the breach at the earliest possible time, and 2) make the effort to rectify the variance from the promises made[93]. By honoring their word and keeping their promises, leaders earn the trust of others.

By keeping their word, leaders demonstrate that they can be counted on.

WDWWSWWD
"We do what we say we will do!"

---

[91] See Collins, J., (2001), *op. cit.* and his discussion of Level 5 Leaders.

[92] *Ibid.*

[93] Caldwell, C., (2018). *Leadership, Ethics, and Trust.* Newcastle upon Tyne, UK: Cambridge Scholars Publishing.

Although trust is difficult to earn, individuals who adopt these eight suggestions and honor their relationships with others merit the commitment and followership of those whom they serve.

CONCLUSION

Although trust is essential for great relationships and effective organizational performance, acquiring trust and building commitment can be extremely difficult. Those who seek to earn trust must work hard to understand its complex nature. As an integrated combination of beliefs, values, and intentions, trust behaviors are the result of a complex inner calculus that is primarily a sub-conscious determination[94]. Wise individuals will work hard to ascertain the perceived psychological contracts --with their accompanying duties and expectations -- to understand how others are motivated. Those factors are also critical to creating high-trust relationships.

> Trust is an elusive quality, often built upon gossamer threads which can easily be destroyed. The importance of understanding trust's contribution to cooperative efforts and stronger relationships makes it paramount that leaders in the transformative era not only understand the elements of trust but develop the skills, character, and insights required to build trust and sustain it.

> TRUST IS A FRAGILE THING. EASY TO BREAK, EASY TO LOSE AND ONE OF THE HARDEST THINGS TO EVER GET BACK.

As those who seek to be trusted endeavor to understand the underlying beliefs, assumptions, and priorities of those with whom they work, that effort will enable them to improve their ability to achieve common goals and create improved relationships. Although the SBM identified herein is a complex and often sub-conscious process by which individuals establish their

---

[94] Creed, W. E. D. & Miles, R. E., (1995), *op. cit.*

personal priorities, understanding that model can enable leaders and others who seek to be trusted to relate more effectively with others – in addition to understanding their own values and beliefs more clearly.

Trust is an elusive quality, often built upon gossamer threads which can easily be destroyed. The importance of understanding trust's contribution to cooperative efforts and stronger relationships makes it paramount that leaders in the transformative era not only understand the elements of trust but develop the skills, character, and insights required to build trust and sustain it. Understanding trust and its important qualities can enable leaders to reach the far side of complexity in relationships with others.

References

Anderson, V. & Caldwell, C., (2018). *Humility as Enlightened Leadership*. Hauppauge, NY: Nova Science Publishers.

Barnard, C. I., (1938). *The Functions of the Executive*. Cambridge, MA: Harvard College.

Business Source Complete found on September 1, 2018 at http://web.b.ebscohost.com/ehost/resultsadvanced?vid=4&sid=8b312c b3-1cc9-4042-b267-42096174f427%40sessionmgr102&bquery=TX+ Trust&bdata=JmRiPWJ0aCZ0eXBlPTEmc2l0ZT11aG9zdC1saXZl.

Block, P., (2013). *Stewardship: Choosing Service Over Self-Interest*. San Francisco, CA: Jossey-Bass.

Caldwell, C., (2018). *Leadership, Ethics, and Trust*. Newcastle upon Tyne, UK: Cambridge Scholars Publishing.

Caldwell, C., Floyd, L. A., Taylor, J and Woodard, B. (2014). "Beneficence as a Source of Competitive Advantage." *Journal of Management Development*, Vol. 33, Iss. 10, pp. 1057-1069.

Caldwell, C. & Hansen, M., (2010). Trustworthiness, Governance, and Wealth Creation." *Journal of Business Ethics*, Vol. 97, Iss. 2, pp. 173-188.

Caldwell, C., Hayes, L., and Long, D., 2010. "Leadership, Trustworthiness, and Ethical Stewardship." *Journal of Business Ethics*, Vol. 96, Iss. 4, pp. 497-512.

Caldwell, C. (2009). "Identity, Self-Deception, and Self-Awareness: Ethical Implications for Leaders and Organizations." *Journal of Business Ethics*, Vol. 90, Supp. 3, pp. 393-406.

Caldwell, C., and Hayes, L., (2007). "Leadership, Trustworthiness, and the Mediating Lens." *Journal of Management Development*. Vol. 26, Iss. 3, pp. 261-278.

Caldwell, C., Bischoff, S. J., and Karri, R. (2002). "The Four Umpires: A Paradigm for Ethical Leadership," *Journal of Business Ethics*, Vol. 36, Iss. 1/2, pp. 153-163.

Christensen, C. M., (2016). *The Innovator's Dilemma: When New Technologies Cause Great Firms to Fail.* Boston, MA: Harvard Business Review Press.

Covey, S. R., (2004). *The 8th Habit: From Effectiveness to Greatness.* New York: Free Press and Brainy Quotes, "Stephen Covey Quotes" found online on September 1, 2018 at https://www.brainyquote.com/quotes/stephen_covey_450798.

Creed, W. E. D. & Miles, R. E., (1995). "Trust in Organizations: A Conceptual Framework Linking Organizational Forms, Managerial Philosophies, and the Opportunity Costs of Controls" in *Trust in Organizations: Frontiers of Theory and Research*, Kramer, R. M. & Tyler, T. (Eds.). Thousand Oaks, CA: Sage Publications, pp. 16-38.

DePree, M., (2004). *Leadership is an Art.* New York: Crown Publishing, p. 11.

Duckworth, A., (2018). GRIT: *The Power of Passion and Perseverance.* New York: Scribners,

Gilligan, C., (2016). *In a Different Voice: Psychological Theory and Women's Development.* Boston, MA: Harvard University Press

Gullett, J., Canuto-Carranco, M., Brister, M., Turner, S., and Caldwell, C. (2009). "The Buyer-Supplier Relationship: An Integrative Model of Ethics and Trust." *Journal of Business Ethics*, Vol. 90, Supp. 3, pp. 329-341.

Hansen, M. T., (2018). *Great at Work: How Top Performers Do Less, Work Better, and Achieve More.* New York: Simon & Schuster.

Hayes, L., Caldwell, C., Licona, B. and Meyer, T. E., 2015. "Follower Behaviors and Barriers to Wealth Creation." *Journal of Management Development*, Vol. 34, Iss. 3, pp. 270-285.

Howe, M. D., (Ed.) (1961). *Holmes–Pollock Letters: The Correspondence of Mr. Justice Holmes and Sir Frederick Pollock, 1874–1932, Two Volumes in One* (2nd ed.), p. 109 found online on September 1, 2018 at https://en.wikiquote.org/wiki/Oliver_Wendell_Holmes_Jr2017 Edelman Trust Barometer found online on September 17, 2018 at https://www.edelman.com/trust2017/,

Kotter, J. P., (2012). *Leading Change with a New Preface by the Author.* Boston, MA: Harvard Business Review Press.

Kouzes, J. M. & Posner, B. Z., (2017). *The Leadership Challenge: How to Make Extraordinary Things Happen in Organizations.* San Francisco, CA: Jossey-Bass.

Mayer, R. C., Davis, J. H. & Schoorman, F. D. (1995). "An Integrative Model of Organizational Trust." *Academy of Management Review*, Vol. 20, Iss. 3, pp. 709-734.

Okpala, C. O., Atwijuka, S., & Caldwell, C., (Working Paper). *"Compassionate Leadership in an Arms-Length World."*

Rousseau, D. M., (1995). *Psychological Contracts in Organizations: Understanding Written and Unwritten Agreements.* Thousand Oaks, CA: Sage Publications.

Rousseau, D. M., (1994). "Violating the Psychological Contract: Not the Exception but the Norm." *Journal of Organizational Behavior.*, Vol. 15, Iss. 3, pp. 245-259.

Senge, P. M., (2006). *The Fifth Discipline: The Art & Practice of the Learning Organization.* New York: Doubleday.

Vroom, V., (1994). *Work and Motivation.* San Francisco, CA: Jossey-Bass.

Weick, K. E. (1993). "The Collapse of Sense-Making in Organizations: The Mann Gulch Disaster." *Administrative Science Quarterly*, Vol. 38, Iss. 4, pp. 628-652.

Chapter 4

TRUSTWORTHINESS
AND TRANSFORMATIVE CHANGE

We live in a time of transformative change. Virtually at every turn the time-honored values of people and organizations have been called into question. Political leaders are frequently held in disdain, business ethics has become an oxymoron, and religious and university leaders are considered out of touch and off base in their thinking. Credibility has become a scarce commodity in a world where employees report that they question the integrity of their leaders and struggle to feel loyalty toward their employers. The overwhelming majority of employees no longer believe that their supervisors have their welfare in mind and many believe that those supervisors will make unethical choices in order to serve their own self-interests.

Trust has plummeted below previous levels because of the pressure on business to cut corners to survive in a global economy characterized by fierce competition and questionable ethical practices. The trustworthiness of those who lead is not only doubted but made the brunt of comedians on the nightly television screen as leaders in even the most hallowed of institutions are victimized by crude jokes, parodies, and bad humor. Confidence in those who lead is a rare commodity and heroes and good examples in many arenas are in short supply.

Credibility has become a scarce commodity in a world where employees report that they question the integrity of their leaders and struggle to feel loyalty toward their employers. The overwhelming majority of employees no longer believe that their supervisors have their welfare in mind and many believe that those supervisors will make unethical choices in order to serve their own self-interests.

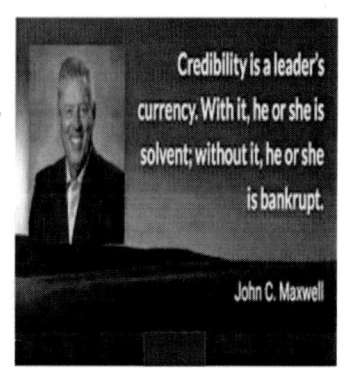

Credibility is a leader's currency. With it, he or she is solvent; without it, he or she is bankrupt.

John C. Maxwell

The trustworthiness of those who lead is not only doubted but made the brunt of comedians on the nightly television screen as leaders in even the most hallowed of institutions are victimized by crude jokes, parodies, and bad humor. Confidence in those who lead is a rare commodity and heroes and good examples in many arenas are in short supply.

The purpose of this chapter is to identify the nature of trustworthiness as that vital concept equates to both individuals and organizations and to identify how both can be perceived as worthy of others' trust. Just as trust in others is a personal commodity measured on a continuum, trustworthiness is subjectively determined and recognized as a critical element in influencing others and to positively influence their willingness to go the extra mile to follow a leader, to cooperate in a team, or to serve their organization. The chapter begins by summarizing key insights from the management literature about the qualities that contribute to trustworthiness – listing twelve different qualities associated with trustworthiness for leaders and organizations. The chapter then relates those qualities to the process of obtaining the commitment and followership of others in today's fast-changing world. We conclude the chapter by offering eight important insights for helping organizations and their leaders to be perceived as trustworthy.

UNDERSTANDING TRUSTWORTHINESS

Trustworthiness is a moral virtue attributing to another party the credibility and reliability to accomplish an intended purpose or shared goal. Implicit in this general definition is the perceiver's belief that the party to be trusted possesses a combination of qualities that enhance that party's ability to act. The following are twelve important qualities for an individual or an organization to be perceived as being trustworthy.

> Trustworthiness is a moral virtue attributing to another party the credibility and reliability to accomplish an intended purpose or shared goal.

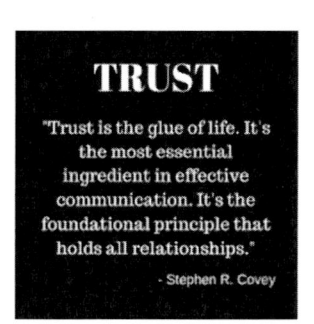

TRUST

"Trust is the glue of life. It's the most essential ingredient in effective communication. It's the foundational principle that holds all relationships."

- Stephen R. Covey

Context – The capacity to understand a situation's context is essential in developing the most effective and appropriate response to a situation, problem or opportunity. Max DePree explained that "the first task of the leader is to define reality[95]." Understanding context enables a leader to assess a situation and to develop the most effective response to achieve a desired outcome[96]. Perspective is always critical in recognizing the importance of context.

---

[95] DePree, M., (2004). *Leadership is an Art*. New York: Crown Publishing, p. 11.
[96] The ability to understand context is a fundamental requirement of Emotional Intelligence. See Goelman, D., (2005). *Emotional Intelligence: Why It Can Matter More than IQ*. New York: Bantam Books.

Candor includes the willingness to confront reality to achieve a worthy purpose -- but candor also requires the ability to speak with the honesty earned by forging a powerful relationship with others.

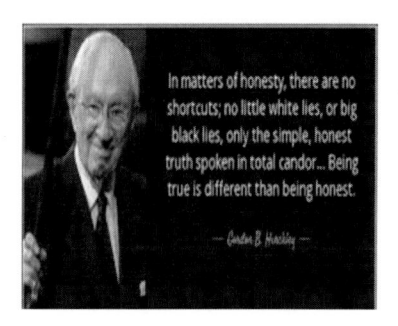

In matters of honesty, there are no shortcuts; no little white lies, or big black lies, only the simple, honest truth spoken in total candor... Being true is different than being honest.

— *Gordon B. Hinckley* —

Candor – Candor is the skill required in providing others with frank and honest feedback, particularly when that feedback is helpful and constructive[97]. Candor's core tenets are about being honest, being direct, but also being respectful[98]. Candor includes the willingness to confront reality to achieve a worthy purpose[99] -- but candor also requires the ability to speak with the honesty earned by forging a powerful relationship with others.

Consideration -- Consideration is often linked with candor, demonstrating the importance of providing honest and candid insights while demonstrating a genuine dedication to others' welfare[100]. How a person presents his or her ideas to others demonstrates their sensitivity to those persons' needs -- including others' readiness to receive information that, given wrongly, might be perceived as hurtful or offensive.

Competence – The technical knowledge about key information, the ability to apply principles in a real-world setting, and the ability to perform tasks required to accomplish key goals are elements of competence required for success in the pursuit of virtually every worthy goal. No important tasks can be accomplished without the competence required, and competence is as important as any other quality in building trust[101].

---

[97] In identifying the importance of candor, Stephen M. R. Covey suggested that it was essential in creating trust. See Eberhardt, N. K., (2013). "Uncommon Candor: Which Comes First? Trust or Candor?" Pathwise Partners, Oct. 25, 2013 found online on October 10, 2018 at http://pathwisepartners.com/blog/which-comes-first-trust-or-candor.

[98] Covey, S. M. R. & Merrill, R. R., (2006). *The SPEED of TRUST: The One Thing that Changes Everything*. New York: Free Press.

[99] *Ibid.*

[100] *Ibid.*

[101] The importance of competence is clearly articulated in Covey, S. R., (1991). *Principle-Centered Leadership*. New York: Simon & Schuster.

The technical knowledge about key information, the ability to apply principles in a real-world setting, and the ability to perform tasks required to accomplish key goals are elements of competence required for success in the pursuit of virtually every worthy goal.

Caring – The demonstrated behaviors associated with the pursuit of the welfare, growth, and wholeness of others are the basis for caring in relationships and exponentially add value in building trust[102]. Caring transcends a benevolent attitude toward others and rises to the level of beneficent behaviors[103] – in much the same way that compassion transcends empathy by converting understanding to action.

Character – The integrity to keep commitments, honor promises, and fulfill ethical duties owed to others is a fundamental requirement of great character and is well-recognized as a critical factor in building trust in relationships[104]. Character is recognized as the basis for personal credibility in leadership relationships and is essential for leaders who wish to be respected by both peers and followers[105].

---

[102] See, for example, Caldwell, C., Hayes, L., and Long, D., (2010). "Leadership, Trustworthiness, and Ethical Stewardship." *Journal of Business Ethics*, Vol. 96, Iss. 4, pp. 497-512

[103] Caldwell, C., Floyd, L. A., Taylor, J and Woodard, B. (2014). "Beneficence as a Source of Competitive Advantage." *Journal of Management Development*, Vol. 33, Iss. 10, pp. 1057-1069.

[104] The classic academic article about trust and trustworthiness is Mayer, R. C., Davis, J. H. & Schoorman, F. D., (1995). "An Integrative Model of Organizational Trust." *Academy Management Review* of. Vol. 20, Iss. 3, pp. 709-734.

[105] Kouzes, J. M. & Posner, B. Z., (2011). *Credibility: How Leaders Gain and Lose It, Why People Demand It.* San Francisco, CA: Jossey-Bass.

Character is recognized as the basis for personal credibility in leadership relationships and is essential for leaders who wish to be respected by both peers and followers.

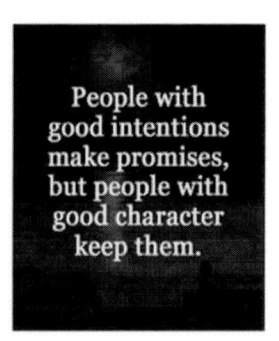

People with good intentions make promises, but people with good character keep them.

Commitment – The degree to which individuals and organizations demonstrate their dedication to principles, to a goal, or to a worthy ideal is measured by commitment. Follower who are asked to be "owners and partners" of an organizational purpose model the behaviors of leaders who model the way and exemplify their commitment[106].

By communicating well, leaders and organizations establish guidelines and ground rules, give important feedback, and share information that is absolutely essential for achieving shared goals.

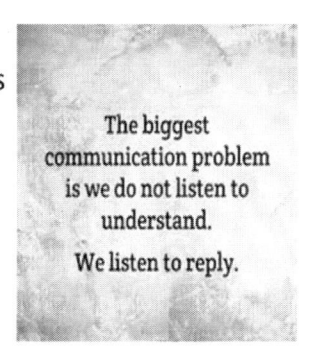

The biggest communication problem is we do not listen to understand.

We listen to reply.

Communication – The skill of being able to communicate effectively includes both listening to others and sharing one's own ideas. Communication is a vital two-way process for creating relationships, for clarifying ideas, for acknowledging the value of others, and for making oneself available. By communicating well, leaders and organizations establish guidelines and ground rules, give important feedback, and share information that is absolutely essential for achieving shared goals[107].

---

[106] Kouzes, J. M. & Posner, B. Z., (2017). *The Leadership Challenge: How to Make Extraordinary Things Happen in Organizations* (6th ed.). San Francisco, CA: Jossey-Bass.
[107] *Ibid.*

Charisma – Those who lead often possess the personality, charm, and ability to connect with others on the personal level. Charisma also refers to a leader's sense of his or her personal calling to accomplish a noble goal or purpose, as well as the ability to inspire within others a fierce sense of personal ownership in joining in the leader's quest. Both qualities enable leaders and organizations to reach others at the emotional level[108].

> By their compliance, leaders model respect for principles and values which are fundamentally important to people and organizations and which benefit the larger group and society.

Compliance – When leaders are compliant with the laws of the land or with the laws of their religious beliefs, they demonstrate their personal obedience to an underlying set of rules or standards of behavior that are shared with those whom they lead. By their compliance, leaders model respect for principles and values which are fundamentally important to people and organizations and which benefit the larger group and society[109].

Capacity – The dynamism required to convert a strategic plan into action is widely regarded as a key quality of effective leaders[110]. Many are the leaders and organizations that develop well-conceived action plans but lack the capacity to translate those plans into action. This unique ability to implement ideas is highly valued.

---

[108] Charisma and its importance in leader-follower relationships are described in Conger, J. A. & Kanungo, R. N., (1998). *Charismatic Leadership in Organizations.* Thousand Oaks, CA: Sage.

[109] See Caldwell, C. and Clapham, S., (2003). "Organizational Trustworthiness: An International Perspective." *Journal of Business Ethics*, Part 1, Vol. 47, Iss. 4, pp.349-364.

[110] The importance of implementation as the distinguishing quality of effective leaders and organizations is identified in Pfeffer, J., (1998). *The Human Equation: Building Profits by Putting People First.* Boston, MA: Harvard Business Review Press.

Leaders who understand that their choices must comply with their inner voice of conscience recognize that their actions and decisions are accountable to a higher standard of ethical duty and responsibility than is commonly recognized.

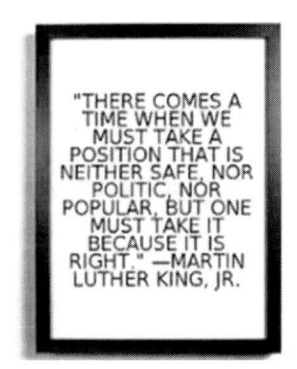

"THERE COMES A TIME WHEN WE MUST TAKE A POSITION THAT IS NEITHER SAFE, NOR POLITIC, NOR POPULAR, BUT ONE MUST TAKE IT BECAUSE IT IS RIGHT." —MARTIN LUTHER KING, JR.

Conscience – Leaders who understand that their choices must comply with their inner voice of conscience recognize that their actions and decisions are accountable to a higher standard of ethical duty and responsibility than is commonly recognized. Leaders and organizations which honor this higher sense of moral responsibility demonstrate that they are truly worthy of others' trust[111].

Each of these twelve qualities is subjectively perceived by every individual in an organization and the decision to trust is based upon each person's cumulative evaluation of a leader or of an organization. Followers make the assessment of a leader or organization's trustworthiness by assessing their own individual priorities for determining whether the person or the organization being evaluated is worthy of their trust. Table 1 identifies how each of the twelve qualities of trustworthiness is applied in evaluating an individual or an organization.

The standards of conduct for individuals and organizations set forth in this table demonstrate that trustworthiness is neither easily obtainable nor readily earned without attention to detail, commitment to excellence, and the willingness to honor obligations to stakeholders in the pursuit of optimal results. Excellence is not easily achieved, but it is always worth the effort.

---

[111] See Covey, S. R., (2004). *The 8ᵗʰ Habit: From Effectiveness to Greatness.* New York: Free Press and Caldwell, C., and Ndalamba, K. K., (2017). "Trust and Being 'Worthy' – The Keys to Creating Wealth." *Journal of Management Development*, Vol. 36, Iss. 8, pp. 1076-1086.

Table 1. Qualities of trustworthiness assessed in leaders and organizations

Trustworthiness Quality	Assessed for Individuals	Assessed for Organizations	Comment
Context	Ability to understand individual needs along with organization goals.	Understanding of organizational priorities and outcomes in a fluid economy.	Conditions about context are constantly evolving as well as interpretation of priorities.
Candor	The degree to which a leader explains factors needing to be addressed at the individual and organization levels.	The quality of information shared with employees to help employees understand urgency in acting.	Timeliness and recognition of changes needing to be made are both critical factors to be addressed.
Consideration	Demonstrated respect and tact in addressing issues to change.	Whether duties owed to stakeholders are respected.	Respect and tactfulness must be balanced and appropriate.
Competence	Personal ability, intelligence, and experience.	Creation of a team that possesses skills required.	The focus is on demonstrated ability to achieve results.
Caring	Leaders must demonstrate that they view employees as people who matter.	Organizations must create systems that demonstrate that their employees matter.	Leadership is a relationship and people must be treated as "Yous" rather than as "Its."
Character	Honoring commitments made and being honest in dealings.	Honoring espoused values and duties owed to society.	Character is largely about "walking the talk" and integrity.
Commitment	Demonstrated passion and perseverance to achieve goals.	Honoring of obligations to stakeholders and mission.	Commitment is largely purpose driven.
Communication	Listening, validating, and acknowledging as well as clarity.	Sharing information and keeping employees informed.	Two-way communication builds trust.
Charisma	Skill in creating personal relationships and inspiring others.	Focus on the worthy ideals and treating people fairly.	Relationships and "calling" are emphasized.
Compliance	Setting an example of honoring the law and its intent.	Honoring the spirit of the law as well as the letter.	Requires an understanding of paper as well as rules.
Capacity	Dynamic ability to translate ideas into action.	Focus on results and constant improvement.	Acknowledgement that success requires constant efforts.
Conscience	Examines what one ought to do to honor one's highest potential.	Creates opportunities for individuals and the company.	Emphasis is on doing what is virtuous and noble.

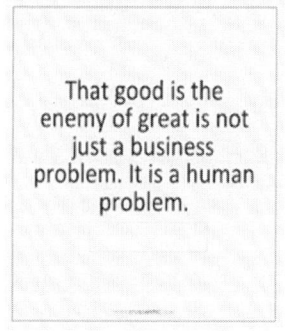

In a world where change is constant and excellence is in constant demand, the qualities of trustworthiness require commitment and standards of excellence that transcend simply being "good." The transformative world of today demands the pursuit of excellence, flexibility, and commitment to constant improvement to be perceived as being trustworthy – whether as leaders or as organizations.

That good is the enemy of great is not just a business problem. It is a human problem.

In a world where change is constant and excellence is in constant demand, the qualities of trustworthiness require commitment and standards of excellence that transcend simply being "good." The transformative world of today demands the pursuit of excellence, flexibility, and commitment to constant improvement to be perceived as being trustworthy – whether as leaders or as organizations. Being worthy of the trust of others requires going beyond simply making a good effort; trustworthiness requires a standard of excellence that demonstrates a fierce commitment to excel[112].

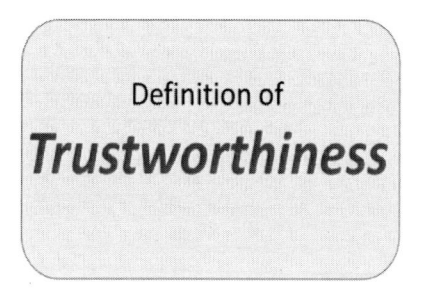

Interpersonal trustworthiness is *an individualized assessment of the probability and degree in which another person will work for one's best interests in pursuing shared goals and honoring duties that is dependent upon the abilities, character, commitment and other qualities of that individual in understanding those duties.*

Definition of **Trustworthiness**

We define interpersonal trustworthiness as *an individualized assessment of the probability and degree in which another person will work*

---

[112] This important point is made in Collins, J., (2001). *Good to Great: Why Some Companies Make the Leap . . .And Others Don't*. New York: HarperCollins.

for one's best interests in pursuing shared goals and honoring duties that is dependent upon the abilities, character, commitment and other qualities of that individual in understanding those duties. The following is a clarifying explanation of key elements of that definition.

Individualized Assessment -- Trustworthiness is subjectively determined by each person through his or her mediating lens. This lens is complex and based upon that individual's core beliefs and ethical perceptions[113].

Probability – The likelihood of another person behaving in a specific manner reflects the uncertainty, risk, and vulnerability that are all associated with trusting that person[114].

Degree – The continuum of personal commitment is measured by behaviors that reflect the extent of personal commitment in a relationship varies from a minimal pro forma contribution to stewardship ownership[115].

Best Interests – Trust is extended based upon the belief that the other party understands one's interests, has the capability to act on one's behalf, and will actually take the required action to benefit the trustor[116].

The assumption is that the parties share a collaborative interest that benefits both individuals. Working together is part of an exchange relationship that unites the parties through a psychological contract of mutual obligation.

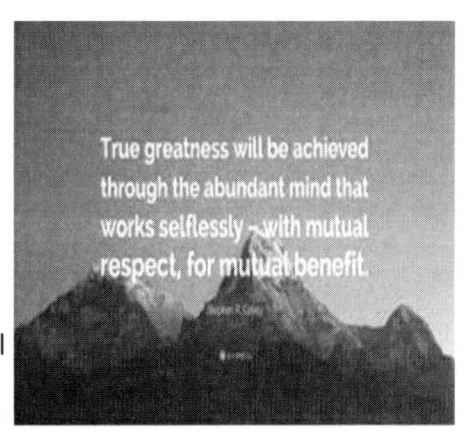

True greatness will be achieved through the abundant mind that works selflessly – with mutual respect, for mutual benefit.

---

[113] Caldwell, C., and Hayes, L., (2007). "Leadership, Trustworthiness, and the Mediating Lens." *Journal of Management Development.* Vol. 26, Iss. 3, pp. 261-278.

[114] Uncertainty, risk, and vulnerability as elements of trust are addressed in Mayer, R. C., Davis, J. H. & Schoorman, F. D., (1995), *op. cit.*

[115] This continuum of commitment is explained in Senge, P. M., (2006). *The Fifth Discipline: The Art & Practice of the Learning Organization.* New York: Doubleday.

[116] These elements of expectancy theory are enumerated in Vroom, V. H., (1994). *Work and Motivation.* San Francisco, CA: Jossey-Bass.

Shared Goals – The assumption is that the parties share a collaborative interest that benefits both individuals. Working together is part of an exchange relationship that unites the parties through a psychological contract of mutual obligation[117].

Honoring – The mutual commitment of trust implies a moral obligation affecting both parties and cooperation together is required to honor the psychological contract[118].

Abilities – The range of abilities incorporates the knowledge, skills, abilities, interpersonal qualities, and capacity to achieve results necessary to perform what is expected[119].

Character – Keeping promises and honoring obligations in a highly ethical manner are obligations reasonably expected in any cooperative relationship and are essential in building trust[120].

Keeping promises and honoring obligations in a highly ethical manner are obligations reasonably expected in any cooperative relationship and are essential in building trust.

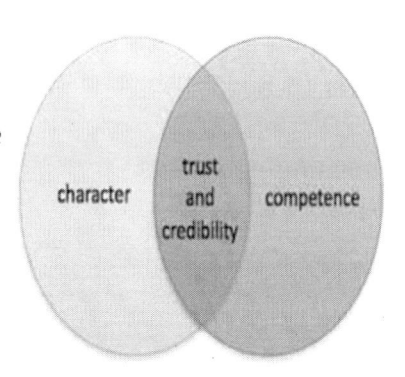

Commitment – If a person who is being trusted lacks the personal commitment or desire to honor an obligation that exists between the parties, the trustor is highly vulnerable and cannot be confident that the other person will perform as expected[121].

---

[117] This relationship is addressed in Rousseau, D. M., (1995). *Psychological Contracts in Organizations: Understanding Written and Unwritten Agreements*. Thousand Oaks, CA: Sage.

[118] *Ibid.*

[119] Mayer, R. C., Davis, J. H. & Schoorman, F. D., (1995), *op. cit.*

[120] *Ibid.*

[121] The importance of this commitment and the consequences associated with failing to honor it are addressed in Reina, D. & Reina, M., (2015). *Trust and Betrayal in the Workplace:*

Other Qualities -- Because the requirements of an interpersonal relationship and the context of a situation may be many and varied, the perceived qualities of the person being trusted may also vary based upon the priorities of the trustor[122].

Understanding – Mutual relationships require mutual understanding and trust is enhanced when the party being trusted articulates his or her commitment to act in the manner understood by the trustor[123].

The responsibilities of the parties are perceived by the trustor as moral duties and obligations and the failure to perform as expected is perceived as an ethical breach.

Duties – The responsibilities of the parties are perceived by the trustor as moral duties and obligations and the failure to perform as expected is perceived as an ethical breach[124].

Each of these respective elements helps to clarify the complex nature of interpersonal trustworthiness and explains why the decision to trust can be so subjective. In a world fraught with constantly evolving variables and the pressure to achieve results, leaders and organizations that recognize the importance of creating high trust and building organization commitment have a vested interest in creating an atmosphere of trust, credibility, and the empowerment of employees.

Building Effective Relationships in Your Organization. San Francisco, CA: Berrett-Koehler Publishers.

[122] Mayer, R. C., Davis, J. H. & Schoorman, F. D., (1995), *op. cit.*

[123] The importance of this mutual understanding is addressed in Rousseau, D. M., (1995), *op. cit.* and Reina, D. & Reina, M., (2015), *op. cit.*

[124] *Ibid.*

At the organizational level, trustworthiness is assessed similar to interpersonal trustworthiness and relates to the expected actions of an organization in creating systems and processes that demonstrate leaders' commitment to the values of trustworthiness and their importance to employees.

Organizational Trustworthiness

At the organizational level, trustworthiness is assessed similar to interpersonal trustworthiness and relates to the expected actions of an organization in creating systems and processes that demonstrate leaders' commitment to the values of trustworthiness and their importance to employees. Research about organizational trustworthiness identified that the nature of organizational trustworthiness is closely related to interpersonal trustworthiness across cultures[125]. Although national cultural factors can profoundly impact differences in values and perceptions[126], research has confirmed that seven important variables significantly affect perceived trustworthiness at the organizational level[127].

Interactional Courtesy: The degree of respect and courtesy shown to others in performing organizational duties.

Responsibility to Inform: The level of communication provided to stakeholders who have an interest in organization objectives and outcomes.

Legal Compliance: The degree to which applicable laws are understood and followed.

---

[125] See, for example, Caldwell, C. and Clapham, S., (2003). "Organizational Trustworthiness: An International Perspective." *Journal of Business Ethics*, Part 1, Vol. 47, Iss. 4, pp.349-364, Caldwell, C., (2004). *Organizational Trustworthiness: A Developmental Model*. Pullman, WA: Washington State University Press, and Xu, B., Xu, F., Caldwell, C., Sheard, G., & Floyd, L., (2016). "Organizational Trustworthiness – Empirical Insights from a Chinese Perspective." *Journal of Management Development*, Vol. 3, Iss. 8, pp. 956-969.

[126] This basic finding is confirmed in Hofstede, G., (2003*). Cultures Consequences; Comparing Values, Behaviors, Institutions, and Organizations Across Nations*. Thousand Oaks, CA: Sage.

[127] These factors were identified in Xu, B., Xu, F., Caldwell, C., Sheard, G., & Floyd, L., (2016), *op. cit.*

Procedural Fairness: The extent to which stakeholders are given the opportunity to participate in fair processes and systems associated with the formal and informal practices of the organization.

Competence: The level of knowledge and ability to achieve results associated with the purpose of an organization.

Financial Balance: The ability of an organization to achieve both efficiency and effectiveness in achieving organization results.

Quality Assurance: The extent to which standards of quality are understood and adhered to on a continuous basis to achieve organization outcomes.

These seven factors overlap with the qualities of interpersonal trustworthiness and affirm the nature of trustworthiness and its similarity at the interpersonal and organizational levels of analysis.

ENHANCING TRUSTWORTHINESS

As individuals and organizations seek to increase how they can be perceived as being more trustworthy in the transformative era, their actions which match the demands of this era can exponentially increase others' perceptions about their worthiness to be trusted. Although the factors that influence perceptions about trustworthiness are individually subjective and often contextually dependent, we suggest eight insights that can enable leaders and organizations to be perceived as worthy of followers' trust.

Embrace Change -- The transformative era is a time of rapid and constant change. That change occurs because information about competitors and customers is virtually instantly available and accessible. The ability to rapidly adapt, to be flexible, and to respond effectively to new expectations and new conditions is absolutely a requirement for competitive success[128].

---

[128] See Christensen, C. M., (2016*). The Innovator's Dilemma: When New Technologies Cause Great Firms to Fail.* Boston, MA: Harvard Business Review Press and Caldwell, C. & Anderson, V., (2018). *Competitive Advantage: Strategies, Management, and Performance.* Hauppauge, NY: Nova Science Publishers.

The inability to change destroys the ability of organizations to compete long-term and undermines customer and employee confidence.

Focusing on what makes up one's unique significance, or what one does at a world class level, is often the key to individual and organizational success.

Prioritize Purpose -- Focusing on what makes up one's unique significance, or what one does at a world class level, is often the key to individual and organizational success[129]. Even though trust behaviors are often in the self-interest of those who are asked to trust, followers are reluctant to give of their best efforts unless they also believe 1) that an organization is committed to achieving a worthy purpose, and 2) that their own personal interests are further by affiliation with that organization. Leaders and organizations who adopt a worthy purpose tend to create high commitment in those with whom they work[130].

Clarify Understanding – The importance of being clear about others' perceptions is especially vital when perceptions involve psychological contracts between the parties[131]. Understanding the other party's point of view and priorities demands high levels of communication skill but earns individuals and organizations credibility while reducing the likelihood of errors and misunderstandings[132].

---

[129] At the individual level, this point is clearly emphasized by Covey, S. R., (2004), *op. cit.* At the organizational level, the importance of focus is described as "The Hedgehog Concept" by Collins, J., (2001), *op. cit.*

[130] Conger, J. A. & Kanungo, R. N., (1998), *op. cit.*

[131] Rousseau. D. M., (1995), *op. cit.*

[132] The ability to "seek first to understand" is advocated in Covey, S. R., (2013). *The 7 Habits of Highly Effective People: Powerful Lessons in Personal Change*. Provo, UT: Stephen R. Covey.

Establishing and honoring meaningful personal relationships is achieved by keeping commitments, demonstrating empathy and compassion, and treating others with dignity and respect.

BE KNOWN FOR YOUR KINDNESS AND GRACE

Honor Relationships – Establishing and honoring meaningful personal relationships is achieved by keeping commitments, demonstrating empathy and compassion, and treating others with dignity and respect. Honoring relationships also includes the ability to recognize when others perceive that a duty is owed to them and acting to ensure that the duty owed is addressed as expected[133].

Empower Authentically – Empowerment is far more than delegating responsibility for a task. Empowerment that is authentic is supportive – providing the training and other resources required to succeed and removing barriers that impede success[134]. Leaders and organizations that assist individuals to succeed and to accomplish important tasks earn the respect of those individuals, as well as their increased efforts.

By demonstrating their commitment to others' welfare and by adopting a servant-leader philosophy, those who guide their organizations effectively demonstrate their commitment to others' success and achieve the organization's success as well.

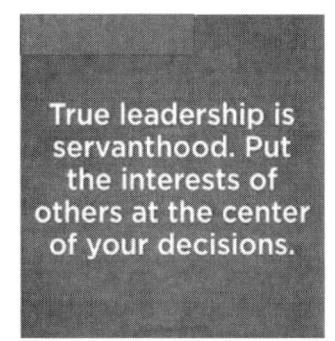

True leadership is servanthood. Put the interests of others at the center of your decisions.

---

[133] Rousseau, D. M., (1995), *op. cit.* and Reina, D. & Reina, M., (2015), *op. cit.*

[134] See Deming, W.E., (2000). *Out of the Crisis*. Cambridge, MA: MIT Press for his description of the obligations of leaders in empowering others.

Emphasize Service – The obligation of those who seek the respect and trust of others is to demonstrate their commitment to others' best interests[135]. In the pursuit of the best interests of their employees and their organizations, the best leaders "choose service over self-interest[136]." By demonstrating their commitment to others' welfare and by adopting a servant-leader philosophy, those who guide their organizations effectively demonstrate their commitment to others' success and achieve the organization's success as well[137].

Improve Constantly – Leaders who demonstrate their commitment to excellence by constantly learning and by improving their own skills are effective at modeling the way for others and exemplify the need to better themselves and their organizations[138]. Coupling this commitment to improvement with the creation of an organization culture that provides ongoing training, develops employees' knowledge and skills, and invests in their constant improvement reinforces employee belief in the importance of continuous improvement and constant learning[139].

A leader's humility in establishing relationships with others generates a response in followers that motivates them to mirror that behavior and builds organization commitment.

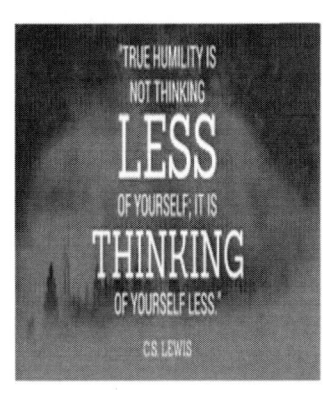

Model Humility – Leaders who take personal responsibility for organization problems and who give credit to others for their organization's

---

[135] DePree, M., (2004), *op. cit.*

[136] This commitment to service is the message of Block, P., (2013). *Stewardship: Choosing Service Over Self-Interest.* San Francisco, CA: Jossey-Bass.

[137] Covey, S. R., (2004), *op. cit.*

[138] Kouzes, J. M. & Posner, B. Z., (2017), *op. cit.*

[139] Senge, P. M., (2006), *op. cit.*

successes demonstrate the personal humility that wins hearts and builds trust[140]. A leader's humility in establishing relationships with others generates a response in followers that motivates them to mirror that behavior and builds organization commitment[141].

These eight behaviors can enable those who seek to be perceived as trustworthy to earn the trust, commitment, and followership of others. Motivated by that trust, organization members are more willing to collaborate, take on extra-mile responsibilities, and dedicate themselves to the success of their organizations and the pursuit of its mission and purpose[142].

THE CHALLENGE

Despite the challenges facing organizations of all types and their leaders, we are fortunate to see outstanding examples of leaders and organizations that establish cultures of high trust and high performance. Trustworthiness is acquired by a leaders' actions and behaviors that demonstrate virtues that inspire others, model the way, and facilitate success[143]. Without that demonstrated trustworthiness, employees withhold commitment, limit their investment in the organization, and protect themselves against the uncertainty of failed promises.

Organizations and their leaders depend upon their ability to be perceived as trustworthy in order to create long-term value and to create the commitment and cooperation so vital for success in the transformative era in which we they now compete. As those who seek to positively influence

---

[140] Collins identified these qualities, coupled with a fierce commitment to achieving results, as the defining characteristics of Level 5 Leaders in Collins, J., (2001), *op. cit.*

[141] See Owens, B, P.; Johnson, M. D. & Mitchell, T. R. (2013). "Expressed Humility in Organizations: Implications for Performance, Teams, and Leadership." *Organization Science*, Vol. 24, Iss. 5, pp. 1517-1538 and Anderson, V. & Caldwell, C., (2018). *Humility as Enlightened Leadership*. Hauppauge, NY: Nova Science Publishers.

[142] Covey, S. R., (2004 & 2013), *op. cit.*

[143] For insights about trust and trustworthiness and their impacts on organizations, see Caldwell, C., (2018). *Leadership, Ethics, and Trust*. Newcastle upon Tyne, UK: Cambridge Scholars Publishing.

others strive to merit their followership and trust, their effectiveness will inevitably be dependent upon their ability to acquire the twelve qualities of trustworthiness and to gain the insights available from demonstrating trustworthy actions.

Organizations and their leaders depend upon their ability to be perceived as trustworthy in order to create long-term value and to create the commitment and cooperation so vital for success in the transformative era in which we they now compete.

Trust

Assured reliance
confidence or faith is pla
the truth, worth, reliabili
dependence on future or
belief in the honesty, int

REFERENCES

Anderson, V. & Caldwell, C., (2018). *Humility as Enlightened Leadership.* Hauppauge, NY: Nova Science Publishers.

Block, P., (2013). *Stewardship: Choosing Service Over Self-Interest.* San Francisco, CA: Jossey-Bass.

Caldwell, C., (2018). *Leadership, Ethics, and Trust.* Newcastle upon Tyne, UK: Cambridge Scholars Publishing.

Caldwell, C. & Anderson, V., (2018). *Competitive Advantage: Strategies, Management, and Performance.* Hauppauge, NY: Nova Science Publishers.

Caldwell, C., Hayes, L., and Long, D., (2010). "Leadership, Trustworthiness, and Ethical Stewardship." *Journal of Business Ethics*, Vol. 96, Iss. 4, pp. 497-512.

Caldwell, C., Floyd, L. A., Taylor, J and Woodard, B. (2014). "Beneficence as a Source of Competitive Advantage." *Journal of Management Development*, Vol. 33, Iss. 10, pp. 1057-1069.

Caldwell, C., and Hayes, L., (2007). "Leadership, Trustworthiness, and the Mediating Lens." *Journal of Management Development.* Vol. 26, Iss. 3, pp. 261-278.

Caldwell, C. and Clapham, S., (2003). "Organizational Trustworthiness: An International Perspective." *Journal of Business Ethics*, Part 1, Vol. 47, Iss. 4, pp. 349-364.

Caldwell, C. and Clapham, S., (2003). "Organizational Trustworthiness: An International Perspective." *Journal of Business Ethics*, Part 1, Vol. 47, Iss. 4, pp. 349-364,

Caldwell, C., (2004). *Organizational Trustworthiness: A Developmental Model.* Pullman, WA: Washington State University Press,

Christensen, C. M., (2016*). The Innovator's Dilemma: When New Technologies Cause Great Firms to Fail.* Boston, MA: Harvard Business Review Press

Collins, J., (2001). *Good to Great: Why Some Companies Make the Leap. and Others Don't.* New York: HarperCollins.

Conger, J. A. & Kanungo, R. N., (1998). *Charismatic Leadership in Organizations.* Thousand Oaks, CA: Sage.

Covey, S. R., (2013). *The 7 Habits of Highly Effective People: Powerful Lessons in Personal Change.* Provo, UT: Stephen R. Covey.

Covey, S. M. R. & Merrill, R. R., (2006). *The SPEED of TRUST: The One Thing that Changes Everything.* New York: Free Press.

Covey, S. R., (2004). *The 8th Habit: From Effectiveness to Greatness.* New York: Free Press and Caldwell, C., and Ndalamba, K. K., (2017). "Trust and Being 'Worthy' – The Keys to Creating Wealth." *Journal of Management Development*, Vol. 36, Iss. 8, pp. 1076-1086.

Covey, S. R., (1991). *Principle-Centered Leadership.* New York: Simon & Schuster.

Deming, W. E., (2000). *Out of the Crisis.* Cambridge, MA: MIT Press.

DePree, M., (2004). *Leadership is an Art.* New York: Crown Publishing, p. 11.

Eberhardt, N. K., (2013). *"Uncommon Candor: Which Comes First? Trust or Candor?"* Pathwise Partners, Oct. 25, 2013 found online on October

10, 2018 at http://pathwisepartners.com/blog/which-comes-first-trust-or-candor.

Goelman, D., (2005). *Emotional Intelligence: Why It Can Matter More than IQ*. New York: Bantam Books.

Hofstede, G., (2003*). Cultures Consequences; Comparing Values, Behaviors, Institutions, and Organizations Across Nations*. Thousand Oaks, CA: Sage.

Kouzes, J. M. & Posner, B. Z., (2011). *Credibility: How Leaders Gain and Lose It, Why People Demand It*. San Francisco, CA: Jossey-Bass.

Kouzes, J. M. & Posner, B. Z., (2017). *The Leadership Challenge: How to Make Extraordinary Things Happen in Organizations* (6th ed.). San Francisco, CA: Jossey-Bass.

Mayer, R. C., Davis, J. H. & Schoorman, F. D., (1995). "An Integrative Model of Organizational Trust." *Academy Management Review* of. Vol. 20, Iss. 3, pp. 709-734.

Owens, B, P.; Johnson, M. D. & Mitchell, T. R. (2013). "Expressed Humility in Organizations: Implications for Performance, Teams, and Leadership." *Organization Science*, Vol. 24, Iss. 5, pp. 1517-1538.

Pfeffer, J., (1998). *The Human Equation: Building Profits by Putting People First*. Boston, MA: Harvard Business Review Press.

Reina, D. & Reina, M., (2015). *Trust and Betrayal in the Workplace: Building Effective Relationships in Your Organization*. San Francisco, CA: Berrett-Koehler Publishers.

Rousseau, D. M., (1995). *Psychological Contracts in Organizations: Understanding Written and Unwritten Agreements*. Thousand Oaks, CA: Sage.

Senge, P. M., (2006). *The Fifth Discipline: The Art & Practice of the Learning Organization*. New York: Doubleday.

Vroom, V. H., (1994). *Work and Motivation*. San Francisco, CA: Jossey-Bass.

Xu, B., Xu, F., Caldwell, C., Sheard, G., & Floyd, L., (2016). "Organizational Trustworthiness – Empirical Insights from a Chinese Perspective." *Journal of Management Development*, Vol. 3, Iss. 8, pp. 956-969.

Chapter 5

STEWARDSHIP AS A TRANSFORMATIVE MODEL

The moral obligation of organizations, from the time of the Greek city-states, has been to create value for society and that moral imperative was required for business owners to be granted the right to practice their trades[144]. Traditionally, the responsibility for governance has been placed on the principals and investors who own the organization and those who serve as its appointed managerial leaders and agents[145]. The evidence suggests that governance is frequently expensive to direct, focused on short-term profits, and struggles to achieve intended results[146] and organizations have struggled their quest to create greater value than their competitors in transforming resources.

Cultural conditions, available assets, environment, and climate -- as well as social, political, and economic factors -- have made that transformation process complicated. The underlying assumptions and philosophies by

---

[144] This obligation is described in Solomon, R. C., (1993). *Ethics and Excellence: Cooperation and Integrity in Business*. Oxford, UK: Oxford University Press. .

[145] Daily, C. M., D. R. Dalton & N. Rajagopalan: (2003). "Corporate Governance: Centuries of Practice, Decades of Research." *Academy of Management Journal*, Vol. 46, Iss. 2, 141-158.

[146] Baucus, M. A. & Beck-Dudley, C. I., (2000). "Designing Ethical Organizations," in *Proceedings*, presented at the International Association for Business and Society (IABS) Annual Meeting, March 2000, Essex Junction, Vermont.

The evidence suggests that governance is frequently expensive to direct, focused on short-term profits, and struggles to achieve intended results and organizations have struggled their quest to create greater value than their competitors in transforming resources.

which decisions are made and organizations are guided have a profound influence on how leaders govern and how successful transformations will be. Understanding the nature of governance and its impact on leading organizations can provide insights about leadership, ethics, and the nature of human relationships that affect the ability to create wealth and add value.

The underlying assumptions and philosophies by which decisions are made and organizations are guided have a profound influence on how leaders govern and how successful transformations will be. Understanding the nature of governance and its impact on leading organizations can provide insights about leadership, ethics, and the nature of human relationships that affect the ability to create wealth and add value.

The purposes of this chapter are 1) to explain the role of stewardship as a philosophy of organizational governance, comparing and contrasting stewardship philosophy with four other governance models with their underlying values and assumptions, and 2) to offer insights as to why a stewardship approach to governance is superior in creating follower trust, achieving desired outcomes, motivating individuals, and creating long-term value for organizations and for society.

We begin by clarifying the role and purpose of organization governance in competing successfully in the modern era. We then identify five established models of organization governance and explain why an ethical stewardship philosophy has six important practical advantages when compared to four other governance approaches. We conclude the chapter by enumerating four important value-based priorities that need to be in place for a stewardship philosophy to be successfully implemented as leaders and organizations seek to increase their ability to create wealth and add value for society.

THE IMPORTANCE OF ORGANIZATIONAL GOVERNANCE

Governance is described as the process by which an organization carries out its operations and incorporates its philosophy about how individuals are most effectively guided, motivated, and directed. Governance includes the systems of authority, control, and accountability that are established to guide an organization as it pursues its purpose, goals, and priorities. Historically, governance focused on the perspectives of owners or principals and the agents hired by firms to manage them, but the importance of the perspectives of employees who work within a firm is also important[147].

Governance is described as the process by which an organization carries out its operations and incorporates its philosophy about how individuals are most effectively guided, motivated, and directed. Governance includes the systems of authority, control, and accountability that are established to guide an organization as it pursues its purpose, goals, and priorities.

---

[147] See Caldwell, C., Karri, R., and Vollmar, P., (2006). "Principal Theory and Principle Theory: Ethical Governance from the Follower's Perspective." *Journal of Business Ethics*, Vol. 66, Iss. 2-3, pp. 207-223,

Traditionally, the responsibility for governance has been placed on the principals and investors who own the organization and those who serve as its appointed managerial leaders and agents[148]. The evidence suggests that governance is frequently expensive to direct, focused on short-term profits, and struggles to achieve intended results[149]. Harvard's Lynn Shar Paine has suggested that governance systems that integrate economic objectives and ethical values are more likely to be sustainable and to achieve superior performance in the new economy[150].

Governance addresses "(1) how an organization is managed to optimize performance and accountability, (2) how values and goals are reflected by the systems and structures that are created, (3) how leaders establish relationships that engender the commitment of those who work with and for them, and (4) how the application of leadership is formally applied in the conduct of organizational business[151]." Ultimately, effective governance demands a connecting relationship between leaders and followers in which those who follow become partners with the organization in the pursuit of shared objectives[152].

Followers in organizations acknowledge the authority of those who lead by cooperating, or relinquishing their control to those who lead, in the pursuit of worthy objectives and to the degree that the organization in which they work addresses and satisfies their individual needs[153]. The degree to which followers relinquish control and demonstrate commitment to an organization and its goals is a key factor in the ultimate success of that

---

[148] Daily, C. M., D. R. Dalton & N. Rajagopalan: (2003). "Corporate Governance: Centuries of Practice, Decades of Research." *Academy of Management Journal*, Vol. 46, Iss. 2, 141-158.

[149] Baucus, M. A.& Beck-Dudley, C. I., (2000). "Designing Ethical Organizations," in *Proceedings*, presented at the International Association for Business and Society (IABS) Annual Meeting, March 2000, Essex Junction, Vermont.

[150] See Paine, L. S., (2002). *Value Shift: Why Companies Must Merge Social and Financial Imperatives to Achieve Superior Performance*. New York: McGraw-Hill.

[151] These four governance purposes are identified on page 178-179 of Caldwell, C., and Hansen, M., (2010). "Trustworthiness, Governance, and Wealth Creation." *Journal of Business Ethics*, Vol. 97, Iss. 2, pp. 173-188.

[152] Coooperrider, D.L. & Sekerka, L.E. (2006). "Toward a Theory of Positive Organizational Change" in Gallos, J.V. (ed.) *Organization Development: A Jossey-Bass Reader*. San Francisco: Jossey-Bass, pp. 223-238.

[153] This point about cooperation was described in 1938 by Chester Barnard. See Barnard, C. I., (1938). *The Functions of the Executive*. Cambridge, MA: Harvard College.

organization in achieving its goals[154] . . . and that cooperative relinquishing of control to a leader is the foundation of trust as well[155].

Traditionally, the responsibility for governance has been placed on the principals and investors who own the organization and those who serve as its appointed managerial leaders and agents. The evidence suggests that governance is frequently expensive to direct, focused on short-term profits, and struggles to achieve intended results.

The degree to which followers relinquish control and demonstrate commitment to an organization and its goals is a key factor in the ultimate success of that organization in achieving its goals . . . and that cooperative relinquishing of control to a leader is the foundation of trust as well.

Implicit in understanding the nature of governance philosophy are seven important factors that each play a major role in influencing the assumptions, values, and guiding principles of those who govern an organization. Each of these factors addresses an important philosophical question about the way in which an organization accomplishes its goals. Table 1 provides a brief summary of each of these seven factors and explains the significance of each factor to organizational governance.

---

[154] This important point is established in Hayes, L., Caldwell, C., Licona, B. and Meyer, T. E., 2015. "Follower Behaviors and Barriers to Wealth Creation." *Journal of Management Development*, Vol. 34, Iss. 3, pp. 270-285 and in Caldwell, C. & Hansen, M., (2010), *op. cit.*

[155] *Ibid.*

Table 1. Factors influencing organization governance

Governance Factor	Philosophical Question	Significance to Governance
Power	Who should be in control?	The assumptions about the right to control are a function of the beliefs about how the best possible decisions are made and whether it is in an owner's interests to be the final decision maker.
Responsibility	What duties do leaders owe an organization?	Whether leaders have an ethical obligation to pursue the best interests of all stakeholders or pursue the best interests of the owners is a key question.
Rights	What rights and values shall be protected?	Owners and leaders have societal obligations as well as duties to employees, investors, and customers.
Priorities	What is the hierarchy of ethical values?	Decisions that are made have multiple consequences and those decisions are inherently based on a priority of values and duties.
Sustainability	How important is the future?	Firms exist within the context of a constantly changing world. Opportunities are never permanent and survival is uncertain.
Accountability	To whom is the firm accountable?	Regulation of the firm is often an internal decision although firms also have a much broader impact on customers, society, and employees.
Efficiency	How should resources best be used?	Firms transform resources to add value and often resources are poorly used or generate harmful by-products.

The philosophy of governance for these seven factors is instrumental, or result-based, and normative, or value-based in its focus and reflects the underlying core beliefs of a firm's principals or owners. These seven factors reflect the owner's philosophies about human nature, ethical duties, and the context in which organizations function.

Typically, owners seek to retain their decision-making *power* because they believe that they have the greatest vested interest in the success of a firm in creating value for which customers are willing to pay. Although owners have much to risk as the provider of capital, organization theory has suggested that "power with" employees generates more effective results and creates greater profits long-term than "power over" others[156]. Modern organizations are acknowledging that the question, "Who should be in control?" in making decisions about customers and their service should involve those employees who are closest to the customer and who best understand their needs[157].

> Organization theory has suggested that "power with" employees generates more effective results and creates greater profits long-term than "power over" others.

The question of *responsibility*, or the duties that leaders owe an organization, is a fundamental issue in organization governance and is monitored closely by the firm's owners or Board of Directors. When a professional leader or agent is hired by the owners, principals, and investors of a firm, the assumption is that this leader has specialized technical knowledge and experience that the owners do not possess and that the leader or agent has a moral duty to pursue the best interests and agenda of those owners. This relationship, however, is one which requires that contractual incentives are created and the agent/leader is carefully monitored to confirm that the owners' agenda and purposes are being accomplished.

By the policies and practices that they adopt, owners communicate the *rights* and values which they espouse for a firm, its members, its customers,

---

[156] This powerful insight was actually suggested nine decades ago by Mary Parker Follett. Follett, M. P., (1927). *Dynamic Administration*. New York: Harper & Bros.

[157] *Ibid.* Follett made this point in her writing and the research of highly regarded scholars have confirmed that the principle is true. See also Pfeffer, J., (1998). *The Human Equation: Building Profits by Putting People First*. Boston, MA: Harvard Business Review Press.

and the communities in which they do business. The reality is that firms often not only seek to limit their obligations to others but sometimes seek to avoid legal obligations. In their quest to be profitable, firms can also engage in self-serving and questionable moral decisions – such as Dutch Shell's track record in failing to avoid oil spills in many parts of the world. Firms also make the decision to get involved in political issues at the local, national, and even the international level to perpetuate their self-interests.

The **priorities** of firms reflect their philosophy of governance and their commitment to the values that they claim.

The *priorities* of firms reflect their philosophy of governance and their commitment to the values that they claim. For example, although Chevron claims that it is deeply committed to protecting the environment the scientific evidence suggests that the company has either delayed in honoring its obligation to clean-up environmental hazards or has consistently avoided acknowledging that they have had an impact for which they are legally responsible. Walmart is another example of a major corporation that has claimed to have a positive impact on consumers yet has had a major negative impact on local businesses and the overall economic health and quality of life of many smaller communities.

Firms often suggest that they are committed to the *sustainability* of society and they embrace their corporate social responsibility. At the same time, many businesses and their owners, investors, and Boards of Directors make decisions that are short-term in their purpose and that often allow them to make quick returns on investment while seriously impairing the future ability of their firm or even future generations to be sustainable long-term. The investment banking, mortgage, and financial management firms exemplify that disregarded that commitment to a sustainable economic marketplace in their manipulation of financial instruments which created the 2008-2009 financial debacle that continues to reverberate throughout the world a decade later[158].

Self-accountability is often considered a "slippery slope" standard for firms who not only make short-term decisions in hopes that their economic health will improve or who fail to validly measure the impact of their decisions on society.

Firm *accountability* is often viewed as a responsibility of government, despite the fact that political machinations over the past thirty years have largely emasculated the ability or desire of governments to regulate businesses whose actions can have a significant impact on people's lives. Political Action groups are commonly formed by major corporations who lobby for their self-interests to avoid being accountable to society or to individuals who are disadvantaged by their actions. Self-accountability is often considered a "slippery slope" standard for firms who not only make short-term decisions in hopes that their economic health will improve or who fail to validly measure the impact of their decisions on society.

Although there are incentives for firms to operate with *efficiency* by reducing waste, improving operations, and limiting their environmental footprint, the unfortunate reality is that firms also know that their own efforts to reduce costs may simply shift the responsibility for the damages that they cause to other parties. A classic case of the decision to minimize costs for Volkswagen was their decision to install a "defeat device" in their diesel vehicles to misrepresent the real amount of pollution of those vehicles when those vehicles were tested. As a result of this pursuit of saving costs short-

---

[158] Friedman, T. L., (2009). *Hot, Flat, and Crowded 2.0 – Why We Need a Green Revolution and How it Can Renew America*. New York: Picador Press.

term, was subject to $35 billion in fines and destroyed its reputation with the public.

MODELS OF ORGANIZATION GOVERNANCE

Five distinctive models or frameworks of organization governance have been established to describe variations in how owners, agents, and organizations interact. These five governance models differ substantially in their focus and emphasis. Table 2 briefly defines each of those five governance models and twelve criteria which distinguish each of the models.

These governance models have their practical examples in the modern organization and each of the five reflects the dominant perspectives of those who make decisions for their organization. The following is a narrative summary of each of the five models.

Agency Theory

In the normal growth pattern of organizations, it is not uncommon for the founders of a firm to recognize that they have come to the point where the continued growth and good health of their company exceeds their level of knowledge and expertise. Principals recognize that continued growth of the firm depends upon hiring agent experts whose specialized technical knowledge and skill sets exceed their own. The agent's specialized competencies put the agent at an advantage in making decisions about the firm and in negotiating a compensation package that benefits him or her at the expense of the firm. If owners of a firm have created an incentive package that protects the agent regardless of firm, the agent may take risks that are personally financially beneficial but that unnecessarily jeopardize the firm. In their quest to bring on board a talented agent, the owners or Board of Directors may provide incentives that create vulnerability to the firm in conflict with their own self-interests.

Table 2. Models of organizational governance

Governance Criteria	Agency Theory	Stakeholder Theory	Stewardship Theory	Principle Theory	Principal Theory
Underlying Assumption	A professional leader can assist a company to maximize wealth creation if given proper incentives.	An organization's wealth creation should be shared by all of its stakeholders and the leader's role is to manage the organization so that the wealth is shared.	The leader optimizes wealth creation long-term by making strategic organization decisions that focus on that objective.	The leader is responsible for ensuring that the driving core principles of the organization are zealously followed.	The leader is responsible for maximizing wealth for the principals or investors and not for other stakeholders.
Leader's Incentive	A contract is created that optimizes the leader's financial interests.	The leader is compensated by his/her ability to satisfy all stakeholders in managing a firm.	The leader seeks long-term value creation that benefits all stakeholders and society.	The leader is compensated for adhering to organization principles.	The leader is compensated for generating value for the owners and investors.
Obligation to Owners	Optimize profits but protect their risk.	Create systems that satisfy stakeholders and perpetuate the firm.	Optimize long-term value creation by adopting wise strategies.	Zealously adhere to defining principles.	Put the owners' interests first in all decisions.
Board of Directors' Role	Create incentives to optimize wealth but limit unreasonable risk.	Monitor organization to ensure that the needs and interests of all stakeholders are addressed effectively	Support decisions that may trade short-term profit-taking but result in long-term value creation.	Monitor compliance with defining principles and values.	Protect the financial interests of the principals and investors over all others.
Employees' Role	Complete tasks to optimize profit creation.	Employees are stakeholders that help create profit.	Employees are owners and partners in creating value and sharing profits.	Employees follow guiding principles in their roles.	Work to produce value for principals.

Table 2. (Continued)

Governance Criteria	Agency Theory	Stakeholder Theory	Stewardship Theory	Principle Theory	Principal Theory
Duty to Employees	Duty is transactional or quid pro quo.	Employees deserve their "fair share" of wealth created.	Optimize value creation so that they can earn maximum benefit.	Teach and emphasize guiding principles.	Quid pro quo relationship.
Ethical Standard	Ethic of economic efficiency.	Ethic is justice-based and focused on "fairness" to all.	Ethic of self-actualization for the firm and its employees.	Ethic is principle-based.	Ethic of self-interest for the principals.
Obligation to Customers	Provide value to ensure continued business	Provide value that enables the firm to continue to be in business.	Optimize value to customers to ensure long-term growth.	Affirm to customers the value of core principles for them.	Meet customer needs to generate profit for principals.
Time Focus	Based upon relationship with leader.	Anticipates a continuing relationship to benefit all stakeholders.	Clearly long-term and focused on increasing value.	Assumes principles have permanent positive affect.	Based upon the principals' agenda. May be short or long.
Major Uncertainty	Will the agent take advantage of superior knowledge?	Can the organization compete most effectively balancing priorities?	To what degree must short-term needs give way to long-term firm priorities?	To what degree are the principles and ideals realistic in today's world?	Will stakeholders act in the principals' best interests as long as required?
Vulnerability	Dependent upon character of agent and incentives offered.	Assumes trad-offs won't jeopardize the firm's ability to compete in a competitive world.	Vulnerable to disruptive innovation and competence of the steward leader.	Dependent upon the practical value of core principles.	Subject to the extent that stakeholder trust can be "bought."
Responsibility to Society	Produce high value products and services,	Produce products and services that can compete in the market.	Improve quality of life and optimize value to ensure long-term success.	Demonstrate importance of principles.	Earn buyer support until principals' needs are satisfied.

Principals recognize that continued growth of the firm depends upon hiring agent experts whose specialized technical knowledge and skill sets exceed their own.

Although the expectation of the owners is that the agent will pursue the owners' best interests in all cases, the "agency problem" occurs when the agent's interests differ from the owners' interests – particularly with regard to risk and vulnerability. The agent may act opportunistically to seek his or her self-interest, a risk called "moral hazard." The primary goal. of the owner in preventing agent self-interest is to provide incentives to make decisions that best benefit the firm in framing the contract between the agent and the owners.

Stakeholder Theory

In Stakeholder Theory, the organization becomes a network of implicit psychological contracts between each stakeholder and the organization with the agent overseeing the contractual relationship with each stakeholder[159]. The ethical premise of this theory is that "the task of management is not only to deal with the various stakeholder groups in an ethical fashion but also to reconcile the conflicts of interest that occur between the organization and the stakeholder groups[160]."

[159] Caldwell, C., and Karri, R. J., (2005). "Organizational Governance and Ethical Systems: A Covenantal Approach to Building Trust." *Journal of Business Ethics*, Vol. 58, Iss. 1, pp. 249-259.

[160] Carroll, A. C. & Brown, J., (2017). *Business and Society: Ethics, Sustainability & Stakeholder Management.* Boston, MA: Cengage,

The premise of stakeholder theory is that its goal is to create value for all of a firm's stakeholders, as opposed to only the shareholders or owners.

Stakeholders each have a stake in the success of a firm, are l beneficiaries of its success, and are dependent upon its survival to achieve their own best interests[161]. The premise of stakeholder theory is that its goal is to create value for all of a firm's stakeholders, as opposed to only the shareholders or owners[162]. The underlying assumption of this theory is that individuals whose organizations share created wealth with all of their stakeholders will be motivated to contribute their best efforts in their own self-interest[163].

The agent has the duty to balance the interests of the owners or principals with the diverse interests of other stakeholders by ensuring that the rights of all stakeholders are acknowledged and by balancing stakeholder interests[164]. Stakeholder Theory seeks outcomes that are procedurally fair and that are based on the agent's ability to reconcile the diversity of interests that arise between stakeholders[165] Inevitably, the frustration of stakeholders within a Stakeholder Theory framework is the feeling that one's interests are compromised, as opposed to being optimized[166].

---

[161] Bonnafous-Boucher , M. & Rendtorff, J. D., (2016). *Stakeholder Theory: A Model for Strategic Management*. New York: Springer.

[162] See Phillips, R. (2003). *Stakeholder Theory and Organization Ethics*. San Francisco, CA: Berrett-Koehler Publishers.

[163] *Ibid.*

[164] This balancing obligation is identified in Smith, H. J. (200). "The Shareholders vs. Stakeholders Debate." *Sloan Management Review,* Vol. 44, Iss. 4, pp. 85-90.

[165] Carroll, A. C. & Brown, J., (2017), *op. cit.*

[166] Caldwell, C., Karri, R., and Vollmar, P., (2006), *op. cit.*

Stewardship Theory

In Stewardship Theory, agents seek to sustain the objectives of the entire organization in seeking to protect and maximize shareholder and organizational wealth[167]. Stewardship Theory perceives that, given the choice between self-serving behavior and pro-social behavior, the steward perceives greater utility in optimizing long-term economic wealth – thereby benefiting the owners and all stakeholders while also maximizing social welfare and long-term economic benefits[168]. The motivation of the steward is morally virtuous and seeks to achieve an ideal future state that benefits all of society[169].

Stewardship Theory perceives that, given the choice between self-serving behavior and pro-social behavior, the steward perceives greater utility in optimizing long-term economic wealth – thereby benefiting the owners and all stakeholders while also maximizing social welfare and long-term economic benefits.

Motivated by a "covenantal" obligation to honor obligations to others, stewards also view employees and other stakeholders as ends in and of themselves, rather than as simply means to the owners' interests[170]. The steward's motivation is to serve multiple stakeholders, thereby benefiting society and optimizing long-term value creation. The steward embraces the notion of "power with" others and acknowledges the wisdom of engaging stakeholders in achieving worthy goals -- including their own self-

---

[167] Davis, J. H., Schoorman, F. D. & Donaldson, L. (1997}. 'Toward a Stewardship Theory of Management." *Academy of Management Review*, Vol. 22, Iss, 1, pp. 20-47.

[168] Caldwell, C., Karri, R., and Vollmar, P., (2006), *op. cit.*

[169] Hernandez, M., (2012). "Toward an Understanding of the Psychology of Stewardship." *Academy of Management Review*, Vol. 37, Iss. 2, pp. 172-193.

[170] *Ibid.*

betterment[171]. In their high regard for others and for society, stewards demonstrate their commitment to normative as well as instrumental priorities[172]. Those priorities earn the steward others' trust and respect because they focus on a commitment to mutual benefit rather than self-interest[173].

Principal Theory

Principal Theory posits that is the principal, the investors, or the owners of a firm that pursue self-interest with guile, rather than the agent[174]. Organizational leaders who view employees entirely from a transactional perspective believe that their ethical obligation end when they pay a quid pro quo salary to employees for their services[175]. This perspective mirrors the idea that Friedman declared in 1970 that the sole purpose of business is to create profits for shareholders[176]

Principal Theory posits that is the principal, the investors, or the owners of a firm that pursue self-interest with guile, rather than the agent.

---

[171] *Ibid.*

[172] *Ibid.*

[173] Hernandez, M., (2008). "Promoting Stewardship Behavior in Organizations: A Leadership Model." *Journal of Business Ethics*, Vol. 80, Iss. 1, pp. 121-128,

[174] Caldwell, C., Karri, R., and Vollmar, P., (2006), *op. cit.*

[175] Burns, J. M., (2010). *Leadership*. New York: Harper Perennial Modern Classics.

[176] Although this article was first published in the *New York Times Magazine* in 1970, it is also found in Friedman M. (2007). "The Social Responsibility of Business Is to Increase Its Profits" in: Zimmerli W. C., Holzinger M., Richter K. (Eds) *Corporate Ethics and Corporate Governance.*, Heidelberg, Germany: Springer, pp. 173-178.

Principal Theory is the consummate example of the ethic of power, wherein principals operate by making decisions to line their own pockets, rather than because their decision benefit their organization and its stakeholders[177]. In so doing, the principals violate their implied obligation create wealth for society and their psychological contract to act in the interests of employees and other stakeholders. Accordingly, governance theory based upon Principal Theory is considered to be trust destroying to society, to customers, and to employees. Unfortunately, there is growing evidence that those who make decisions on behalf of their firms are increasingly perceived to be acting in their own short-term self-interest, rather in the long-term benefit of society or their employees.

Principle Theory is a governance framework based upon the belief that overriding "guiding principles" or values are paramount in governing an organization[178]. Those principles are so dominating that they are emphasized to the point where they are out of balance with the long-term needs of the organization and its stakeholders[179]. An agent is hired to oversee the organization and to conduct its business in compliance with the dominating principles.

Implicit in this theory is the assumption that the guiding principles are so important that they override other organizational priorities – rising to the level of standards which are paramount in society and supersede other principles and values. Organization founders are zealous advocates of the guiding principles and the agent is typically a "true believer" as well. Often organization members are also deeply committed to the organization, its goals, and its dominant principles and the participants view themselves as fulfilling a "calling." The trust of employees and other stakeholders is often tied to a charismatic relationship with the owners, agents, or leaders within the organization.

---

[177] Caldwell, C., Karri, R., and Vollmar, P., (2006), *op. cit.*
[178] *Ibid.*
[179] *Ibid.*

Implicit in this theory is the assumption that the guiding principles are so important that they override other organizational priorities – rising to the level of standards which are paramount in society and supersede other principles and values

The Stewardship Theory model distinguishes itself from the other four theories of governance based upon its commitment to the shared interests of the stakeholders to optimize long-term value creation rather than to be satisfied with a short-term creation and division of wealth. The agent leader's focus is on honoring obligations to society as an important stakeholder – including duties owed to future generations that may be affected by an organization's decisions. The Stewardship Theory model excels at earning the trust of others because of its balanced commitment to stakeholders' best interests, its devotion to the purposes and values upon which an organization is based, its recognition of the importance of empowering and best utilizing stakeholder abilities, and its moral superiority in seeking to create both long-term and short-term value for society.

The Stewardship Theory model excels at earning the trust of others because of its balanced commitment to stakeholders' best interests, its devotion to the purposes and values upon which an organization is based, its recognition of the importance of empowering and best utilizing stakeholder abilities, and its moral superiority in seeking to create both long-term and short-term value for society.

ADOPTING A STEWARDSHIP APPROACH

The governance of organizations according to a Stewardship model requires the ability to understand and apply principles that match today's transformative context. The ability to adapt to change, to be innovative and creative, and to meet the needs of stakeholders with widely varying perspectives and agendas demands a unique combination of skills that are aligned with Stewardship Theory. In this section we identify four important value-based priorities that are essential in implementing Stewardship as a governance philosophy.

A Commitment to Excellence

Stewardship demands that leaders and employees at all levels of an organization are committed to excelling. Optimizing long-term value creation requires constant attention to detail, the ability to implement new methods and technologies, and a clear understanding of customers and their needs. Constant learning and continuous improvement must characterize an organization and its membership must be dedicated to finding new and better ways to address customer priorities. Value creation is ultimately a measure which customers define and organizations must understand present and future customer priorities.

Optimizing long-term value creation requires constant attention to detail, the ability to implement new methods and technologies, and a clear understanding of customers and their needs.

Honoring of Others

Stewardship transcends self-interest and acknowledges that greatness is achieved by honoring relationships with others. Leaders recognize the covenantal nature of their responsibilities and pass on to employees that commitment to society's best interests while simultaneously honoring duties owed to those same employees. By treating others as valued ends and never as means to a larger purpose, stewardship demonstrates its respect for the worth and value of individuals as well as the needs of the larger community and society.

Stewardship transcends self-interest and acknowledges that greatness is achieved by honoring relationships with others.

Dedication to Values

Stewards conform to the values of their organization and demonstrate by their actions that they are authentic leaders. They create systems, policies, and processes that affirm those values in the way that stakeholders are treated and they model what they believe. This alignment of leaders' behaviors and the values that they espouse communicates that leaders have integrity and that they hold others in the organization to their same high standards.

This alignment of leaders' behaviors and the values that they espouse communicates that leaders have integrity and that they hold others in the organization to their same high standards.

Ferocity of Effort

Stewards have a clear vision of the importance of what they are striving to accomplish and use that understanding to motivate their actions. There is no question of the degree of their commitment to the organization, to its mission and purpose, or to the importance of its members and leaders willingly go the extra mile to demonstrate that commitment. Stewards willingly dedicate themselves to what they are striving to accomplish because they fundamentally believe in its essential importance and its benefits to others.

There is no question of the degree of their commitment to the organization, to its mission and purpose, or to the importance of its members and leaders willingly go the extra mile to demonstrate that commitment.

By adopting these four priorities, leaders who embrace the underlying principles of Stewardship Theory demonstrate their worthiness to be trusted by others and their commitment to creating a better organization and a healthier world.

CONCLUSION

The ability of leaders and organizations to create value for society demands that they adopt a governance philosophy that has the ability to unite others in the pursuit of a worthy purpose. Inevitably, those who lead must demonstrate that they not only have the capacity to add value and create wealth but that they understand the implicit responsibilities that they owe to those with whom they labor – and to the larger community.

Inevitably, those who lead must demonstrate that they not only have the capacity to add value and create wealth but that they understand the implicit responsibilities that they owe to those with whom they labor – and to the larger community.

Every business organization is required to make a profit as it transforms resources and delivers products and services that serve others. How leaders govern and the underlying philosophy of their governance models play a significant role in whether those leaders are able to earn the trust and followership of those with whom they work. Stewardship Theory as a governance model demonstrates the values and commitment to excellence that earn the trust of others and merits the thoughtful consideration of principals and agents as they contemplate how to govern in today's transformative era.

REFERENCES

Barnard, C. I., (1938). *The Functions of the Executive*. Cambridge, MA: Harvard College.

Baucus, M. A. & Beck-Dudley, C. I., (2000). "Designing Ethical Organizations," in *Proceedings, presented at* the *International Association for Business and Society (IABS) Annual Meeting*, March 2000, Essex Junction, Vermont.

Bonnafous-Boucher, M. & Rendtorff, J. D., (2016). *Stakeholder Theory: A Model for Strategic Management*. New York: Springer.

Burns, J. M., (2010). *Leadership*. New York: Harper Perennial Modern Classics.

Caldwell, C., and Hansen, M., (2010). "Trustworthiness, Governance, and Wealth Creation." *Journal of Business Ethics*, Vol. 97, Iss. 2, pp. 173-188.

Caldwell, C., Karri, R., and Vollmar, P., (2006). "Principal Theory and Principle Theory: Ethical Governance from the Follower's Perspective." *Journal of Business Ethics*, Vol. 66, Iss. 2-3, pp. 207-223,

Caldwell, C., and Karri, R. J., (2005). "Organizational Governance and Ethical Systems: A Covenantal Approach to Building Trust." *Journal of Business Ethics*, Vol. 58, Iss. 1, pp. 249-259.

Carroll, A. C. & Brown, J., (2017). *Business and Society: Ethics, Sustainability & Stakeholder Management*. Boston, MA: Cengage,

Coooperrider, D. L. & Sekerka, L. E. (2006). "Toward a Theory of Positive Organizational Change" in Gallos, J. V. (ed.) *Organization Development: A Jossey-Bass Reader*. San Francisco: Jossey-Bass, pp. 223-238.

Daily, C. M., D. R. Dalton & N. Rajagopalan: (2003). "Corporate Governance: Centuries of Practice, Decades of Research." *Academy of Management Journal*, Vol. 46, Iss. 2, 141-158.

Davis, J. H., Schoorman, F. D. & Donaldson, L. (1997). "Toward a Stewardship Theory of Management." *Academy of Management Review*, Vol. 22, Iss, 1, pp. 20-47.

Follett, M. P., (1927). *Dynamic Administration*. New York: Harper & Bros.

Friedman, T. L., (2009). *Hot, Flat, and Crowded 2.0 – Why We Need a Green Revolution and How it Can Renew America*. New York: Picador Press.

Friedman M. (2007). "The Social Responsibility of Business Is to Increase Its Profits" in: Zimmerli W. C., Holzinger M., Richter K. (Eds) *Corporate Ethics and Corporate Governance.*, Heidelberg, Germany: Springer, pp. 173-178.

Hayes, L., Caldwell, C., Licona, B. and Meyer, T. E., 2015. "Follower Behaviors and Barriers to Wealth Creation." *Journal of Management Development*, Vol. 34, Iss. 3, pp. 270-285 and in Caldwell, C. & Hansen, M., (2010), *op. cit.*

Hernandez, M., (2012). "Toward an Understanding of the Psychology of Stewardship." *Academy of Management Review*, Vol. 37, Iss. 2, pp. 172-193.

Hernandez, M., (2008). "Promoting Stewardship Behavior in Organizations: A Leadership Model." *Journal of Business Ethics*, Vol. 80, Iss. 1, pp. 121-128,

Paine, L. S., (2002). *Value Shift: Why Companies Must Merge Social and Financial Imperatives to Achieve Superior Performance.* New York: McGraw-Hill.

Pfeffer, J., (1998). *The Human Equation: Building Profits by Putting People First*. Boston, MA: Harvard Business Review Press.

Phillips, R. (2003). *Stakeholder Theory and Organization Ethics*. San Francisco, CA: Berrett-Koehler Publishers.

Smith, H. J. (200). "The Shareholders vs. Stakeholders Debate." *Sloan Management Review,* Vol. 44, Iss. 4, pp. 85-90.

Solomon, R. C., (1993). *Ethics and Excellence: Cooperation and Integrity in Business*. Oxford, UK: Oxford University Press.

Chapter 6

TRANSFORMATIVE PHILOSOPHY AND WHY IT MATTERS – A NEW MORAL PERSPECTIVE

The decline in moral values in the United States has been chronicled by scholars, religious leaders, and politicians for more than half a century[180]. In many hearts, moral relativism and short-term self-interest seeking have replaced the commitment to honoring responsibilities to others -- including obligations owed to future generations[181]. Inevitably, the root cause of the decision to pursue opportunistic self-interest is the absence of a conscious sense of the consequences of individual action. That gap in acknowledging the impacts of one's choices often results from the failure of individuals to define and to commit themselves to a guiding philosophy associated with their personal identities. The disturbing result of that failure to define one's personal philosophy is that it is not uncommon for people to find themselves on a path that conflicts with the type of person that they really would like to become.

---

[180] See, for example, Schoedinger, A. (2004). *Where Have All Our Values Gone? The Decline of Values in America and What We Can Do About It?* Bloomington, IN: Xlibris Publishing.

[181] This critique of a world value system is the subject of Friedman, T. L., (2009). *Hot, Flat, and Crowded: Why We Need a Green Revolution – And How It Can Renew America, Release 2.0.* New York: Penguin.

The disturbing result of that failure to define one's personal philosophy is that it is not uncommon for people to find themselves on a path that conflicts with the type of person that they really would like to become.

Developing a guiding philosophy is not a simple task. That task requires a thoughtful assessment of what one values, how a person views her or his own identity, what (s)he wishes to contribute to the world, and how they define the purpose of life. Although we each may unconsciously address those important issues, our failure to formally define our own philosophy of life may lead to the incremental decisions that result in the disappointing reality that we do not like who we have become.

Our failure to formally define our own philosophy of life may lead to the incremental decisions that result in the disappointing reality that we do not like who we have become.

In reality, other people liking you is a bonus. You liking yourself is the real prize.

The purpose of this chapter is to propose that leaders who seek to become more effective at earning the trust and followership of others can achieve that goal by developing a Transformative Philosophy to guide their lives. A Transformative Philosophy is a new concept that incorporates the high standards of ethical leadership and service to others. A Transformative Philosophy enables leaders to honor their obligation 1) to pursue long-term wealth creation, 2) to benefit society, 3) to improve organizations, and 4) to assist colleagues to become the best version of themselves. We begin the chapter by defining what it means to be transformative. We then explain the six key elements of Transformative Philosophy – including in that explanation the contribution of each element to building follower commitment and trust. We then offer seven specific suggestions that can assist individuals to develop a meaningful personal Transformative Philosophy. We conclude the chapter with a challenge to individuals to apply those suggestions in their quest to become more effective leaders.

DEFINING TRANSFORMATIVE

For decades, leadership experts have called for leaders to adopt a new and higher standard – a transformative standard that raised the bar of the leader's commitment to society, to organizations, to followers, and to become their very best selves.

For decades, leadership experts have called for leaders to adopt a new and higher standard – a transformative standard that raised the bar of the leader's commitment to society, to organizations, to followers, and to become their very best selves. James McGregor Burns called for a leadership model that transcended old transactional relationships with employees and honored the obligation to serve others and to help them to become their best. Stephen Covey called upon leaders to find their own voice, or unique significance, and then treat others so well that they not only recognize their highest potential but strive to achieve it.

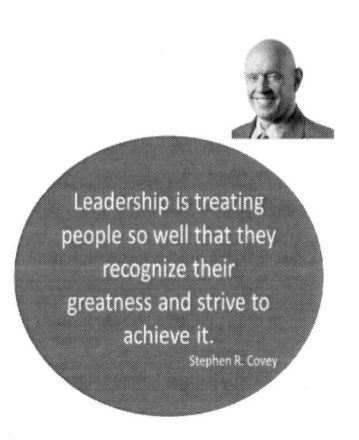

Stephen Covey called upon leaders to find their own voice, or unique significance, and then treat others so well that they not only recognize their highest potential but strive to achieve it.

Leadership is treating people so well that they recognize their greatness and strive to achieve it.
Stephen R. Covey

That which is "transformative" has been described as including eight specific characteristics that reinforce productive change[182].

Committed to Change

That which is transformative is committed to continuous improvement in a world that is characterized by constant change. Change is viewed as a positive opportunity to benefit society and to serve others.

Responsive to Customers

Responding to customers and assisting them to achieve their goals is essential for creating long-term customer relationships. Understanding customer needs means knowing what they are striving to accomplish in a competitive world.

---

[182] These eight characteristics come from Caldwell, C. & Hooper, H., (2018). "A Transformative Philosophy: Insights to Excellence" in *Human Resource Management: A Transformative Approach*, Caldwell, C. & Anderson, V. (Eds.) Hauppage, NY: NOVA Publications, Chapter Three and from Caldwell, C., Hooper, H., and Atwijuka, S., (2018(. "Transformative Philosophy: A Leadership Approach to Achieving Excellence." *Open Journal of Human Resource Management*, Vol 1, Iss. 1, pp. 53-56 and available online at http://www.sryahwapublications.com/open-journal-of-human-resource-management/volume-1-issue-1.

Learning Focused

Constantly improving related knowledge, technical skills, insights about the business industry, and evolving technology required to perform effectively are mandatory. Creating a learning culture includes encouraging experimentation and innovation in addition to improving efficiency.

Creating a learning culture includes encouraging experimentation and innovation in addition to improving efficiency.

Externally Adaptive

Organizations must recognize constantly adapt to new technology, unexpected economic conditions, competitor innovation, and other factors that affect the external context of their business. Managing change demands that leaders and organizations assess these external factors.

Internally Integrated

An organization's systems, processes, and practices of an organization must integrate with an organization's values, goals, and purpose to optimize its ability to accomplish the results necessary to succeed. Internal integration demands that leaders understand the ways that structures, systems, and policies impact day-to-day employee efforts.

Ethically Virtuous

Ethical standards must be fully incorporated into an organizational culture and leaders must exemplify those standards in order for those standards to be accepted and adopted. What is virtuous seeks to achieve the best possible outcomes.

Dynamically Capable

Translating good ideas and a well-conceived strategy into action are the defining skills that determine the difference between an opportunity and a reality. The quality of being dynamically capable is a rare quality essential in managing any transition.

Translating good ideas and a well-conceived strategy into action are the defining skills that determine the difference between an opportunity and a reality. The quality of being dynamically capable is a rare quality essential in managing any transition.

Consistently Focused

Successful organizations focus their efforts on that which they do extremely well. They understand what is necessary to be successful, they are purpose driven, and they strive to avoid wasting resources on activities that are unproductive.

These eight criteria are each important in managing transformative change and are necessary to achieve results that transcend the commonplace.

By incorporating these eight characteristics, leaders and organizations respond to the increasing demands of customers and improve their ability to compete successfully in the modern economy[183].

ELEMENTS OF TRANSFORMATIVE PHILOSOPHY

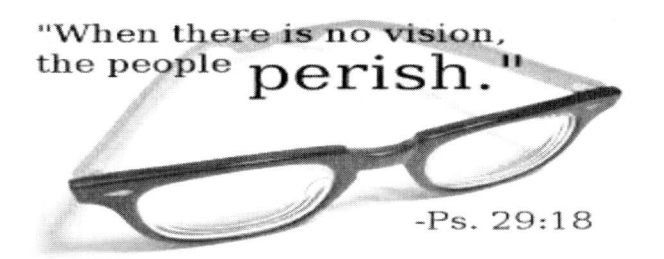

"When there is no vision, the people **perish.**"

-Ps. 29:18

The Proverbs declare, "Where there is no vision, the people perish[184]." The capacity to understand life's purpose, the insight to recognize one's ideal role in life, and the integrity to take the steps to fulfill one's highest potential are three key elements of vision. Leadership vision and the capacity to utilize that vision to guide one's life are key requirements for developing a personal moral philosophy which can provide clarity when individuals feel overwhelmed and a philosophy can serve as a touchstone for decision-making during times of high stress[185]. Indeed, a philosophy encompasses one's vision of what (s)he ought to be and how (s)he should devote his or her life.

A new and more effective approach to solving problems was called for by Albert Einstein who declared that "(t)he significant problems we face cannot be solved at the same level of thinking with which we created them[186]." Developing better solutions to solving problems enables firms to

---

[183]Caldwell, C. & Anderson, V., (2017). *Competitive Advantage: Strategies, Management, and Performance*. Hauppage, NY: NOVA Publications.

[184] This Biblical reference is found in Proverbs 29:18.

[185] Ndalamba, K. K., Caldwell, C. & Anderson, V., 2018. "Leadership Vision as a Moral Duty." *Journal of Management Development*, Vol. 37, Iss. 3, pp. 309-319.

[186] Einstein's famous quote has been cited in many ways. The idea behind it however is constant.

create a competitive advantage and provides individuals with an advantage over others who rely on old ways of thinking about issues[187].

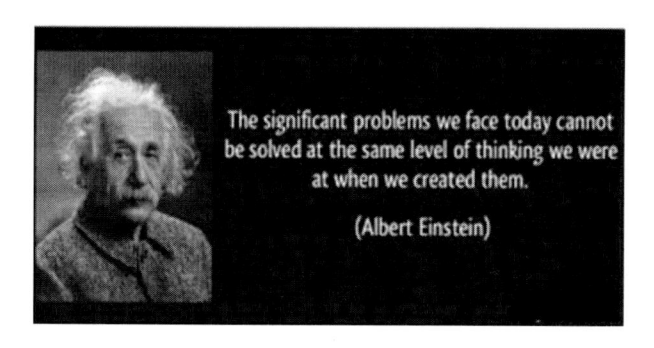

James McGregor Burns advocated a new approach to transforming leadership thinking, calling for a "transformative" change to empowering and engaging others, as opposed to traditional top-down thinking and a transactional relationship with employees.

Transformative Change

Over the years, many experts have also called for transforming old ways of thinking to add new value and the paradigms used for making decisions and assessing opportunities have evolved as experience and better information have built upon faulty assumptions previously held[188]. James McGregor Burns advocated a new approach to transforming leadership thinking, calling for a "transformative" change to empowering and engaging

---

[187] This insight is provided by Covey, S. R., (1992). *Principle-Centered Leadership*. New York: Fireside Press.

[188] See, for example, Kolsky, E., (2014). "New Paradigms Bring Value to Knowledge Management." *CRM Magazine*, Vol. 15, Iss. 10, pp. 40-41.

others, as opposed to traditional top-down thinking and a transactional relationship with employees[189].

Six Elements of Philosophy

Transformative Philosophy has been defined as "an ethically-based way of thinking, feeling, and interacting that earns the respect, trust, and commitment of others by effectively aligning purpose, principles, policies, people, practices, and priorities in the constant pursuit of long-term value creation and performance excellence." This definition serves to frame the six key components of a Transformative Philosophy within an organization in establishing a framework for adapting to change, delivering services to customers, and competing within its industry. Philosophy incorporates the six components, identified in Figure 1 below.

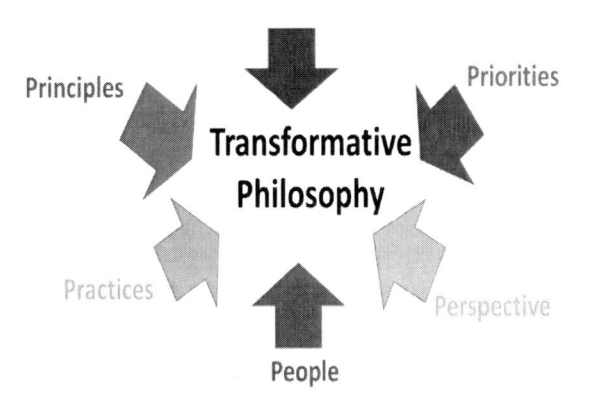

Figure 1. A model of transformative philosophy.

Each of these six components contribute to a Transformative Philosophy that enables a leader to serve stakeholders and achieve optimal results. The following is a summary of each of these six components.

---

[189] This point about the need for a new transformative approach to leadership was made in Burns, J. M., (1978) *Leadership*. New York: Harper & Row Publishers.

Purpose

The key question addressed by any organization is, "Why is our work important?"

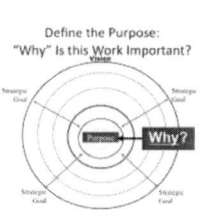

The purpose and mission of an organization is its reason for being. Organizations that emphasize being excellent at what they are doing are more profitable than comparable companies that emphasize maximizing profits[190]. The key question addressed by any organization is, "Why is our work important?" The organizational purpose is an essential factor for employees joining an organization and is essential in keeping employees committed to their work[191]. Organizational purpose is a fundamental requirement for leaders to maintain organizational followership and trust[192].

Principles

The universal principles, values and assumptions about people and organizations are the foundation upon which a philosophy is based. Principles affirm the commitment of organizational leaders to the standards and values of the organization[193]. Principles incorporate universal standards that are acknowledged to have practical application across many contexts[194]. A philosophy is based upon guiding principles which serve as the moral and

---

[190] Collins, J. & Porras, J. I., (2004). *Built to Last: Successful Habits of Visionary Companies*. New York: Harper Business.

[191] The importance of organizational purpose is emphasized in the classic by Chester Barnard. See Barnard, C. I., (1938). *The Functions of the Executive*. Cambridge, MA: Harvard College.

[192] *Ibid.*

[193] Schein, E. H. & Schein, P., (2016). *Organizational Culture and Leadership* (5th ed.). San Francisco, CA: Jossey-Bass.

[194] Covey, S. R., (1992). *Principle-Centered Leadership*. New York: Fireside Press.

ethical foundation of an organization and those principles and values are also viewed as important in building trust[195].

The universal principles, values and assumptions about people and organizations are the foundation upon which a philosophy is based. Principles affirm the commitment of organizational leaders to the standards and values of the organization.

Practices

Practices are the policies, and procedures that are implemented by an organization and are incorporated in the systems and structures of the organization. These policies reflect the consistency of an organization's philosophy and values[196]. Practices, systems, and values must be aligned as part of an organization's philosophy if they are to create the high commitment and high performance necessary for the accomplishment of organization goals[197]. The alignment of practices or the lack thereof confirms the consistency of organization leaders and earns or loses follower respect.

The alignment of practices or the lack thereof confirms the consistency of organization leaders and earns or loses follower respect.

---

[195] Schein, E. H. & Schein, P., (2016), *op. cit.*

[196] *Ibid.*

[197] Beer, M., (2009). *High Commitment High Performance: How to Build a Resilient Organization for Sustained Advantage*. San Francisco, CA: Jossey-Bass.

People

Research has confirmed that the quality of people in an organization are the determining factor in its ability to acquire and retain a competitive advantage[198]. A firm's philosophy for hiring and compensating employees reflects its philosophy about people and their importance. Investing in people through employee training and development is also acknowledged to be a critical factor of successful organizations[199]. Companies that demonstrate that employees are highly valued communicate that commitment by establishing employee engagement programs, compensating employees based upon their performance, and involving employees in decisions that affect their work[200]. The way that employees are treated largely determines how they feel about the organization.

Research has confirmed that the quality of people in an organization are the determining factor in its ability to acquire and retain a competitive advantage.

Perspective

Perspective is the overall outlook that individuals and organizations have about the nature of the world and how people and organizations interact. A firm that believes that it has an obligation to society and to the

[198] Collins, J., (2001). *Good to Great: Why Some Companies Make the Leap . . . And Others Don't.* New York: HarperCollins.

[199] Pfeffer, J., (1998). *The Human Equation: Building Profits by Putting People First.* Boston, MA: Harvard Business Review Press.

[200] Beer, M., (2009), *op. cit.*

communities that it serves applies that perspective in the ways that it honors obligations environmentally and economically[201]. Organizations that create high commitment and high trust reinforce the belief that employee potential is much higher than other organizations typically believe[202].

Perspective is the overall outlook that individuals and organizations have about the nature of the world and how people and organizations interact.

Priorities

Priorities reflect what the leaders of a firm believe matters most. They also identify what is expected in conducting personal relationships, and define the criteria for making decisions[203]. Research conducted in several studies confirmed, for example, that many leaders believe that their first priority is to hire outstanding individuals[204]. Other studies argue that the process that a company uses to make decisions, especially in innovating new ideas, is a critical priority that differentiates successful from unsuccessful organizations[205]. As companies communicate their priorities and then honor what they claim to believe, they reinforce their trustworthiness in the minds of their employees[206].

---

[201] Friedman, T. L., (2009), *op. cit.*

[202] Beer, M., (2009), *op. cit.*

[203] See, for example, Hosmer, L. T., (2010). *The Ethics of Management* (7th ed.). Boston, MA: McGraw-Hill Education.

[204] Collins, J., (2001), *op. cit.*

[205] Collins, J. & Hansen, M. T., (2011). *Great by Choice: Uncertainty, Chaos, and Luck – Why Some Thrive Despite Them All*. New York: HarperBusiness.

[206] Schein, E. H. & Schein, P., (2016), *op. cit.*

Priorities reflect what the leaders of a firm believe matters most.

These six components interrelate as organization leaders establish the underlying assumptions and standard which define their organization philosophy. Unfortunately, it is typically the case that organization leaders emphasize economic goals and define their purpose in terms of a company's competitive position, rather than upon the values and principles of a formal philosophy.

DEVELOPING A TRANSFORMATIVE PHILOSOPHY

A Transformative Philosophy requires a specific mindset and a set of assumptions about individuals, organizations, and society. Although a Transformative Philosophy has identifiable advantages in today's fast-changing economic world, there are inherent conflicts between that philosophy and many common assumptions about management and leadership. For that reason, we include seven suggestions for individuals considering whether their mental models fit with the requirements of a Transformative Philosophy.

1. *Adopt a Servant Leader Perspective.* The assumption that leaders can be effective with a top-down, high-control, management approach is inconsistent with a transformative approach.

The assumption that leaders can be effective with a top-down, high-control, management approach is inconsistent with a transformative approach.

Effective Leadership:
More Than Just the Boss

2. *Extend Communication Organization-wide.* Engaging and empowering employees is vital to creating the high trust essential for successful transformation. Sharing information and communicating with employees at all levels is a necessity in building trust.

3. *Focus on Collaboration and Cooperation.* Building internal competition amongst employees and among departments is inherently inconsistent with a transformative model. Instead, emphasize creating partnerships in solving problems requiring input from many perspectives.

4. *Coach Rather than Judge.* Performance evaluation and performance appraisal systems should focus on helping employees to succeed, rather than on identifying their shortcomings. The supervisor relationship should emphasize helping employees to become their best.

Performance evaluation and performance appraisal systems should focus on helping employees to succeed, rather than on identifying their shortcomings.

5. *Make Flexibility the Standard.* Resistance to change is the enemy to transformative success. Emphasize the importance of a constantly evolving, constantly improving, and constantly learning organization.

6. *Invest in People.* That investment is far more than an economic investment and must be a personal commitment to each individual's welfare, growth, and wholeness. Employees become "owners and partners" of an organization's agenda when they are treated as valued individuals.

> Recognize that employees want to be part of an organization that truly adds value to the world, rather than simply producing wealth for stakeholders.

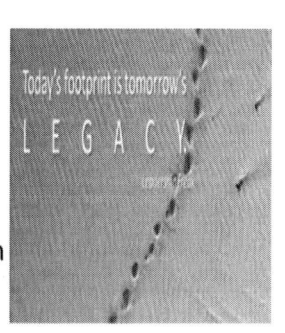

7. *Emphasize the Legacy.* Recognize that employees want to be part of an organization that truly adds value to the world, rather than simply producing wealth for stakeholders. Make the purpose of the organization and its role in society a daily part of the organization's culture. Focus the organization on the importance of constantly improving and honoring its moral and ethical responsibilities. Keep the organization focused on a noble purpose, honoring duties to others, and creating a better world.

Accepting the Challenge

It would be naïve and inaccurate to suggest that being successful in the modern economy is an easy task, or even that a company's long-term success was based upon whether its leaders had adopted the elements of a

Transformative Philosophy. Acknowledging that reality, we nonetheless challenge corporate leaders to pay close attention to the six components of a Transformative Philosophy and that they consider the seven suggestions associated with adopting that philosophy.

The distinguishing elements of a Transformative Philosophy are its sense of moral purpose and its vision of our obligation as citizens of a larger community.

Today's employees have made it clear that they are dissatisfied with present day leaders and the lack of integrity that is typical of so many leaders and organizations in the modern world. The distinguishing elements of a Transformative Philosophy are its sense of moral purpose and its vision of our obligation as citizens of a larger community. Eighty years ago, in one of the most cited business books ever written Chester Irving Barnard opined that organizations were only successful if 1) they accomplished a worthy purpose, and 2) if they benefited their individual members[207]. A Transformative Philosophy contains the crucial elements that can enable today's leaders and organizations to reestablish trust with their employees and reinvigorate flagging businesses in today's troubled economic times.

REFERENCES

Barnard, C. I., (1938). *The Functions of the Executive*. Cambridge, MA: Harvard College.

---

[207] Barnard, C. I., (1938) *The Functions of the Executive*. Cambridge, MA: Harvard College.

Beer, M., (2009). *High Commitment High Performance: How to Build a Resilient Organization for Sustained Advantage*. San Francisco, CA: Jossey-Bass.

Burns, J. M., (1978) *Leadership*. New York: Harper & Row Publishers.

Caldwell, C. & Hooper, H., (2018). "A Transformative Philosophy: Insights to Excellence" in *Human Resource Management: A Transformative Approach*, Caldwell, C. & Anderson, V. (Eds.) Hauppauge, NY: Nova Science Publishers, Chapter Three

Caldwell, C., Hooper, H., and Atwijuka, S., (2018). "Transformative Philosophy: A Leadership Approach to Achieving Excellence." *Open Journal of Human Resource Management*, Vol 1, Iss. 1, pp. 53-56 and available online at http://www.sryahwapublications.com/open-journal-of-human-resource-management/volume-1-issue-1.

Caldwell, C. & Anderson, V., (2017). *Competitive Advantage: Strategies, Management, and Performance*. Hauppauge, NY: Nova Science Publishers.

Collins, J. & Hansen, M. T., (2011). *Great by Choice: Uncertainty, Chaos, and Luck – Why Some Thrive Despite Them All*. New York: Harper Business.

Collins, J. & Porras, J. I., (2004). *Built to Last: Successful Habits of Visionary Companies*. New York: Harper Business.

Collins, J., (2001). *Good to Great: Why Some Companies Make the Leap. and Others Don't*. New York: HarperCollins.

Covey, S. R., (1992). *Principle-Centered Leadership*. New York: Fireside Press.

Friedman, T. L., (2009). *Hot, Flat, and Crowded: Why We Need a Green Revolution – And How It Can Renew America, Release 2.0*. New York: Penguin.

Hosmer, L. T., (2010). *The Ethics of Management* (7th ed.). Boston, MA: McGraw-Hill Education.

Kolsky, E., (2014). "New Paradigms Bring Value to Knowledge Management." *CRM Magazine*, Vol. 15, Iss. 10, pp. 40-41.

Ndalamba, K. K., Caldwell, C. & Anderson, V., 2018. "Leadership Vision as a Moral Duty." *Journal of Management Development*, Vol. 37, Iss. 3, pp. 309-319.

Pfeffer, J., (1998). The Human Equation: Building Profits by Putting People First. Boston, MA: *Harvard Business Review* Press.

Schein, E. H. & Schein, P., (2016). *Organizational Culture and Leadership* (5th ed.). San Francisco, CA: Jossey-Bass.

Schoedinger, A. (2004). *Where Have All Our Values Gone? The Decline of Values in America and What We Can Do About It?* Bloomington, IN: Xlibris Publishing.

Chapter 7

STEWARDSHIP AS A MORAL VIRTUE

The University of Michigan's Kim Cameron has emphasized that great leaders are both responsible and virtuous[208]. Cameron equated responsible leadership with virtuousness – a leadership standard transcending accountability and dependability by enhancing moral relationships and the pursuit of excellence[209]. Virtuousness "focuses on elevating, flourishing, and enriching outcomes" in "pursuit of humanity's very best qualities[210]." The pursuit of the highest and best of one's capabilities – the capacity to "find one's voice" or unique significance and to achieve the best possible version of oneself -- is the ideal that is sought for by both great leaders and the best organizations[211].

The purposes of this chapter are 1) to explain the importance of the pursuit of the superlative as the fundamental characteristic of ethical stewardship, 2) to explain why leaders who adopt a stewardship model of governance honor the highest standards of ethical leadership, 3) to identify why the stewardship approach to serving individuals and organizations

---

[208] See Cameron, K., (2011). "Responsible Leadership as Virtuous Leadership." *Journal of Business Ethics*, Vol. 98, pp. 25-35.

[209] *Ibid.*

[210] *Ibid.* p. 25.

[211] Stephen R. Covey makes this point in defining leadership and in describing the ultimate purpose of organizations in Covey, S. R., (2004). *The 8th Habit: From Effectiveness to Greatness.* New York: Free Press, pp. 98-99.

enables leaders to be perceived as morally virtuous. Although the stewardship approach to organization governance has been identified as a positive framework for leadership in the past[212], this chapter identifies in greater detail why ethical stewardship inspires greater follower trust, increased employee commitment, and the extra-mile dedication required for firms to be competitive in today's global marketplace.

Virtuousness "focuses on elevating, flourishing, and enriching outcomes" in "pursuit of humanity's very best qualities." The pursuit of the highest and best of one's capabilities – the capacity to "find one's voice" or unique significance and to achieve the best possible version of oneself -- is the ideal that is sought for by both great leaders and the best organizations.

Kim Cameron

We begin the chapter with a brief review of the nature of stewardship and its underlying commitment to long-term wealth creation. We then identify the nature of both masculine and feminine morality, primarily citing the work of Lawrence Kohlberg[213] and Carol Gilligan[214] who are most frequently identified as responsible for defining those two moral models. After identifying the highest standards of morality emphasized by both models, we clarify how stewardship integrates the best qualities of both

---

[212] Examples of those who have written about stewardship and its importance include Morela Hernandez and Peter Block. See Hernandez, M., (2008). "Promoting Stewardship Behavior in Organizations." Journal of Business Ethics, Vol. 80, Iss. 1, pp. 121-128, Hernandez, M., (2012). "Toward an Understanding of the Psychology of Stewardship." *Academy of Management Review*, Vol. 37, Iss. 2, pp. 172-193, and Block, P., (2013). *Stewardship: Choosing Service Over Self-Interest*. San Francisco, CA: Jossey-Bass.

[213] Kohlberg, L., (1981). *The Philosophy of Moral Development: Moral Stages and the Idea of Justice*. New York: Harper & Row.

[214] Gilligan, C., (2016). *In a Different Voice: Psychological Theory and Women's Development*. Boston, MA: Harvard University Press.

masculine and feminine morality while also addressing the extremely high standards of Transformative Ethics. We conclude the chapter by identifying five virtuous qualities of stewardship that demonstrate why leaders who adopt that standard of governance are perceived as morally virtuous.

UNDERSTANDING STEWARDSHIP

Morela Hernandez

Perhaps the most insightful way to describe the nature of stewardship is to view the concept from the perspective offered by the University of Virginia's Morela Hernandez. Hernandez described the psychology of stewardship and the underlying motivations which form the basis upon which stewards act. Benefiting from Hernandez's thoughtful paper we briefly summarize eight underlying assumptions implicit in stewardship[215].

Covenantal Commitment – Stewardship reflects "an ongoing sense of obligation or duty to others based on the intention to uphold the covenantal relationship[216]." A covenantal commitment is a leader's recognition of his or her obligation to honor the responsibility to not only serve others but to help them to constantly seek out the truth, to become their best, and to help others to also thrive[217].

---

[215] For a complete understanding of Hernandez's contributions, see Hernandez, M., (2012), *op. cit.*
[216] *Ibid.*, p. 174.
[217] The nature of Covenantal Leadership is described in Pava, M., (2003). *Leading with Meaning: Using Covenantal Leadership to Build a Better Organization.* New York: St. Martin's Press.

Covenantal Commitment

A covenantal commitment is a leader's recognition of his or her obligation to honor the responsibility to not only serve others but to help them to constantly seek out the truth, to become their best, and to help others to also thrive.

Collective Benefit – Stewardship distinguishes between that which benefits individuals, including oneself, and those actions which have a collective benefit. The stewardship obligation acknowledges and differentiates between individual self-serving options and choices that optimize the best interests of all participants[218].

Collective Benefit

The stewardship obligation acknowledges and differentiates between individual self-serving options and choices that optimize the best interests of all participants.

Service over Self-Interest

Long-Term Orientation – Stewardship recognizes that short-term benefits may actually undermine the best interests of others long-term. Hernandez emphasizes that stewards understand the importance of choices that impact the future as well as the immediate situation[219].

---

[218] This same point is emphasized by Block, P., (2013), *op. cit.*
[219] Hernandez, M., (2012), *op. cit.*

Long-Term Orientation

Stewardship recognizes that short-term benefits may actually undermine the best interests of others long-term.

Relationship-Centered -- Leaders who are stewards establish relationships and influence others' actions by emphasizing "a high degree of collaboration and a significant level of autonomy and responsibility[220]". Stewardship acknowledges the importance of people as valued ends, rather than as the means to accomplish a leader's goals[221].

Relationship-Centered

Stewardship acknowledges the importance of people as valued ends, rather than as the means to accomplish a leader's goals.

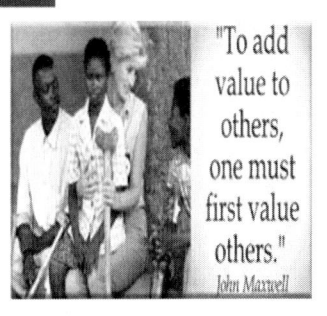

"To add value to others, one must first value others."
John Maxwell

Shared Responsibility -- Individuals who are empowered, share influence, and "behave with autonomy but collectively share responsibility for work outcomes that can affect multiple stakeholders[222]." This sharing of responsibility increases ownership, individual commitment, and personal obligation.

---

[220] *Ibid.*, p. 178.
[221] Covey, S. R., (2004), op. cit.
[222] Hernandez, M., (2012), p. 178.

Shared Responsibility

Individuals who are empowered, share influence, and "behave with autonomy but collectively share responsibility for work outcomes that can affect multiple stakeholders."

Morela Hernandez

Intrinsically Rewarding – Stewardship promotes self-efficacy by providing growth opportunities that enhance others' personal competencies. Stewardship also increases self-determination by enabling participants to make individual contributions that are intrinsically rewarding.

Intrinsically Rewarding

Stewardship promotes self-efficacy by providing growth opportunities that enhance others' personal competencies. Stewardship also increases self-determination by enabling participants to make individual contributions that are intrinsically rewarding.

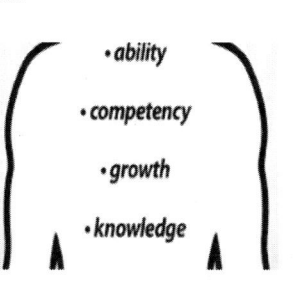

- *ability*
- *competency*
- *growth*
- *knowledge*

Other Regarding -- Stewardship willingly sacrifices self-interest in the service of others[223] and demonstrates a moral regard for contributing to social welfare and the needs of multiple stakeholders. The steward's identity is validated by the value of the worth of the contribution made[224].

---

[223] Block, P., (2013), *op. cit.*
[224] Hernandez, M., (2012), *op. cit.*

Other Regarding

Stewardship willingly sacrifices self-interest in the service of others and demonstrates a moral regard for contributing to social welfare and the needs of multiple stakeholders.

Affective Connection – Both personal commitment and emotional connection with team members are enhanced by the stewardship process. Affective affiliation with the organization and shared feelings with colleagues enhance personal responsibility and psychological ownership of the goals of an organization[225].

Affective Connection

Affective affiliation with the organization and shared feelings with colleagues enhance personal responsibility and psychological ownership of the goals of an organization.

THE OWNERSHIP EFFECT

Rising to the level of a sacred responsibility, stewardship honors the desire to create a better world, to build a great organization, and to empower oneself and others to become self-actualized individuals. In the pursuit of long-term value creation, stewards demonstrate their commitment to accomplishing superlative results – and this commitment to greatness defines the stewardship agenda and earns the respect and commitment of others.

---

[225] *Ibid.* Hernandez emphasizes the importance of this ownership as a key element of stewardship.

MORAL PERSPECTIVES AND STEWARDSHIP

According to the *Stanford Encyclopedia of Philosophy*, the concept of morality is addressed in two distinct ways[226]:

1. Descriptively to refer to certain codes of conduct put forward by a society or a group (such as a religion), or accepted by an individual for her own behavior, or
2. Normatively to refer to a code of conduct that, given specified conditions, would be put forward by all rational persons.

Two Approaches to Morality

- Descriptively to refer to certain codes of conduct put forward by a society or a group (such as a religion), or accepted by an individual for her own behavior, or

- Normatively to refer to a code of conduct that, given specified conditions, would be put forward by all rational persons.

Kohlberg's model is a framework describing the evolution of moral reasoning in assessing behaviors. The assumption of the model is that each successive stage builds upon the previous stage and that the sixth stage reflects the greatest maturity in moral development.

The bias, of course, of the respective advocates of the codes of conduct advocates as moral is that their code is rational and applicable. The intention of every moral code is to provide a standard to guide individual lives and to serve as a touchstone for conduct in society.

---

[226] Gert, B. & Gert, J. (2017) "The Definition of Morality." In *The Stanford Encyclopedia of Philosophy*, Edward N. Zalta (ed.), and found online on October 18, 2018 at https://plato.stanford.edu/archives/fall2017/entries/morality-definition/>.

Lawrence Kohlberg's theory of moral development[227] is frequently described as a masculine code of conduct, inasmuch as it was developed by studying the behavior and moral reasoning of young men and is considered to be a rules-oriented and rational model emphasizing a fairness and justice perspective toward morality[228]. In contrast, Carol Gilligan conducted a study of how women viewed moral conduct and obligations[229]. Gilligan's Ethic of Care approach to morality reflects a distinctly feminine code of conduct based upon relationships, responsibility, caring, and compassion[230]. These two somewhat contrasting perspectives about moral conduct are briefly summarized.

KOHLBERG'S MODEL OF MORAL DEVELOPMENT

Building upon the work of Piaget, Kohlberg sought to identify the developmental stages of moral development by testing the responses of young boys to a series of scenarios about which he sought to obtain the underlying rationale for which they made decisions. Based upon their responses, developed a model of moral development based upon three levels with two stages within each level[231].

Level One: Pre-Conventional Morality

The focus of this level is egocentric and is centered on the anticipated consequences of action.

---

[227] See Kohlberg, L., (1981), *op. cit.*
[228] Zizek, B., Garz, D. & Nowak, E., (Eds.), (2015). *Kohlberg Revisited*. Rotterdam, The Netherlands: Sense Publications.
[229] Gilligan, C., (2016), *op. cit.*
[230] *Ibid.*
[231] See Kohlberg, L., (1981), *op. cit*

Stage 1 – Obedience and Punishment

The motivation at this stage is to obey and comply in order to avoid a possible punishment.

Stage 2 – Self-Interest

Choices are made which serve one's self-interest or personal benefit and are often viewed as a *quid pro quo* exchange.

Level Two: Conventional Morality

Morality of actions is based upon societal views about what is appropriate and conventional.

Stage 3 – Conformity and Interpersonal Accord

Behavior fits with social norms. The motivation is to be perceived aa a "good person."

Stage 4 – Maintaining Authority and Social Order

Motivation is derived from outside forces, such as the legal system, which dictate the requirements for social order.

Level Three: Post Conventional Morality

Morality of behaviors is determined by principles and transcends societal views when human rights are concerned.

Stage 5 – Social Contract Driven

Laws are not rigid but reflect the social contract to benefit society. Individuals should be respected for the right to a difference of opinion. Decisions are made by compromise and majority opinion.

Stage 6 – Universal Ethical Principles

Laws are valid to the degree that they comply with social justice. Universal principles should govern behavior and actions should be based upon the standard of "what is right."

Kohlberg's model is a framework describing the evolution of moral reasoning in assessing behaviors. The assumption of the model is that each successive stage builds upon the previous stage and that the sixth stage reflects the greatest maturity in moral development[232].

GILLIGAN'S MODEL OF MORAL DEVELOPMENT

Gilligan was a research associate of Kohlberg and argued that women viewed moral development from a different perspective than men. Gilligan explained that women view relationships as the basis for responsibilities and moral duties[233]. Rather than focusing moral decisions on the just and fair option which were the basis for Kohlberg's model, Gilligan found that women place primary importance on a caring response that demonstrates compassion for others[234].

Gilligan's moral model, like Kohlberg's, also adopted the three major levels which she also labeled pre-conventional, conventional, and post conventional. Unlike Kohlberg, however, Gilligan suggested that the transitions between stages of moral development reflected changes in self-identity rather than cognitive moral development. In contrast with Kohlberg's reliance upon Piaget's cognitive developmental model, Gilligan's based her model on a modified version of Freud's theories about ego development[235].

The stages of development in Gilligan's Ethic of Care identify three levels of ego development which she proposed[236]

---

[232] *Ibid.*
[233] Gilligan, C., (2016), *op. cit.*
[234] *Ibid.*
[235] *Ibid.*
[236] These three stages are described in Howard, T., (2018). "Carol Gilligan Theory: How Women Develop Their Sense of Self." Betterhelp found online on October 19, 2018 at

Gilligan suggested that the transitions between stages of moral development reflected changes in self-identity rather than cognitive moral development. In contrast with Kohlberg's reliance upon Piaget's cognitive developmental model, Gilligan's based her model on a modified version of Freud's theories about ego development,

Pre-Conventional

Gilligan's model of preconventional morality is based on an individual's perceived need to survive. The fundamental motivation in this stage is focused on choosing to meet one's own needs before meeting the needs of others.

Conventional

Conventional morality is related to the understanding that there is good in self-sacrifice for the benefit of others. Persons in this stage obtain satisfaction in viewing themselves as good by assisting others to meet their basic needs rather than concentrating entirely on their own needs.

Post-Conventional

Post-conventional morality advocates that there should be a way for people to meet their own needs without hurting others -- whether in caring for others or for oneself.

---

https://www.betterhelp.com/advice/psychologists/carol-gilligan-theory-how-women-develop-their-sense-of-self/.

Gilligan explained that two moral development transitions occur which are based upon changes in one's sense of self. In the pre-conventional stage, people are primarily focused on caring about how they can satisfy their own needs. The first transition happens when individuals begin to understand their role in also caring for the needs of others. In the second transition, occurring between the conventional and post-conventional stages, the focus evolves to emphasizing being good, making virtuous choices and focusing on what is morally true. In this second transition, choices evolve consistent with 1) an inner light defining truth and morality, 2) one beliefs about what is universally true, and 3) what benefits the world overall in the long term[237].

STEWARDSHIP AND THE TWO MORALITIES

Stewardship encompasses the best qualities of both the masculine and feminine moralities. Stewardship's focus on achieving optimal results, its conformance with correct principles, and its dedication to fairness support Kohlberg's masculine criteria. The steward's commitment to long-term priorities, to treating people as valued partners, and to honoring covenantal responsibilities demonstrates stewardship's adherence to Gilligan's feminine model of moral development. Figure 1 is a pictorial portrayal of the overlap between the best qualities of Kohlberg's and Gilligan's models, demonstrating how both of those moral perspectives are incorporated into the stewardship approach to governance.

This overlap between Kohlberg's and Gilligan's moral development models offers insights into the value of a stewardship framework that incorporates the defining qualities of both moral development models. As importantly, the steward's commitment to the high standards of morality of both the masculine and feminine perspectives demonstrates the steward's commitment to the highest moral standards of both perspectives.

---

[237] *Ibid.*

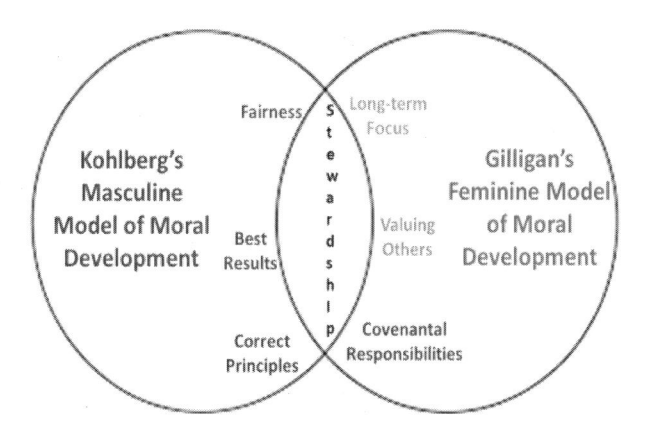

Figure 1. Stewardship's and masculine and feminine morality.

STEWARDSHIP AND TRANSFORMATIVE ETHICS

As a model of governance stewardship fits within the ethical standards of Transformative Ethics (TE), a new ethical framework that encompasses the ethical priorities of twelve other well-regarded and often-cited ethical perspectives[238]. When TE was introduced, in 2017, the authors of that new model defined TE as "an integrative model of ethical stewardship" as a defining characteristic of TE. Table 1 briefly summarizes the twelve contributing perspectives of TE and clarifies their ethical significance[239].

As a model of governance stewardship fits within the ethical standards of Transformative Ethics, a new ethical framework that encompasses the ethical priorities of twelve other well-regarded and often-cited ethical perspectives.

---

[238] See Caldwell, C., and Anderson, V. "Transformative Ethics: An Integrative Model of Ethical Stewardship." A working draft of a paper presented at the International Academy of Management and Business Conference in New Orleans, Louisiana on January 20, 2017.
[239] Ibid., p. 13.

Table 1. Twelve contributing ethical perspectives to transformative ethics

Ethical Perspective	Contributing Ideal	Ethical Virtue	Value to Transformative Ethics
Ethic of Self-Interest	*"Pursue outcomes which have the greatest positive benefit for oneself and one's organization without infringing upon the rights of others."*	Balanced Self-Interest	Acknowledges that value creation is important and self-interest is beneficial, but that others have rights that must also be honored.
Virtue Ethics	*"Constantly pursue excellence, make that pursuit a habit, and treat others with integrity."*	Commitment to Excellence	Confirms that to be honorable and to develop habits of excellence are requisites as personal standards.
Ethic of Religious Injunction	*"Always treat others with dignity, respect, and kindness – as valued 'Yous' and never as anonymous 'Its.'"*	Authentic Understanding	Demands that others be treated with kindness, compassion, and empathy at all times.
Ethic of Government Regulation	*"Live by both the letter and the spirit of the law in honoring duties owed to others, but remember that the law by itself is a minimal moral standard."*	Genuine Compliance	Confirms that the purpose of rules must always be taken into account and that the intent of those rules is as critical as or more important than the letter.
Utilitarian Ethics	*"No actions should be engaged in which do not result in the greatest good for that community of which you are a part."*	Value Optimization	Affirms that this greatest good is both outcome-oriented and rights-oriented in creating value – with an obligation to minimize any possible harm.
Ethic of Universal Rules	*"Act according to universal principles and rules which you would have others apply if they were in your similar situation and your positions were reversed."*	Just Action	Treats others as they wish to be treated and complies with universally-understood principles that benefit mankind.

Ethical Perspective	Contributing Ideal	Ethical Virtue	Value to Transformative Ethics
Ethic of Universal Rights	*"No one, including governments, may take action that infringes upon the legitimate rights of any other individual."*	Guaranteed Rights	Honors basic human rights and ensures that those rights may not be infringed upon – even under color of claim for a public benefit.
Ethic of Economic Efficiency	*"Achieving an efficient use of resources to create value for society is a virtuous goal."*	Efficient Use	Conserves and efficiently uses scarce resources and acknowledges that efficient and effective value creation benefits society.
Ethic of Distributive Justice	*"Act only in ways that acknowledge the rights, liberty, and equality of all and take no actions that harm the least among us."*	Honor Everyone	Recognizes that, though justice is a multi-faceted construct, no actions should be taken that harm those who are disadvantaged in society.
Ethic of Contributing Liberty	*"Take no actions which impede the self-development or self-fulfillment of others."*	Self-fulfillment	Promotes the liberty which allows all individuals to pursue self-development and self-fulfillment and acknowledges that society benefits thereby.
Ethic of Self-Actualization	*"Seek to discover your innate greatness and fulfill that potential to create a better world."*	Discovered Greatness	Emphasizes the innate talents, gifts, and highest potential of individuals and their responsibility to use those talents productively to make a better world.
Ethic of Care	*"Respect others as valued individuals, share concern for their welfare, and honor the responsibility to treat each person with empathy and compassion."*	Care Authentically	Affirms the responsibility to care for others' best interests and to treat them with love and with demonstrated concern for their welfare and wholeness.

TE adopts "the philosophy of the ethical steward and seeks the highest standard of ethical and moral performance[240]". Each of the values of TE correlate with stewardship priorities and the duties that stewards owe to others. Figure 2 shows the twelve ethical perspectives of TE and their relationship to stewardship.

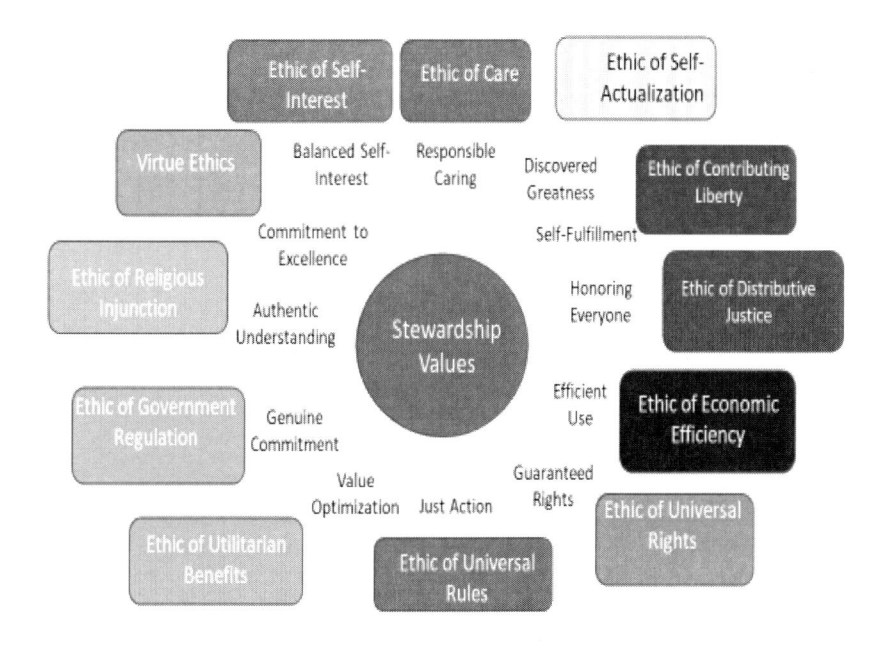

Figure 2. Ethical perspectives of transformative ethics and stewardship.

Stewardship's belief that self-improvement, personal development, and character development are not only possible but fundamental requirements of great leadership fits perfectly with the moral commitment of TE[241]. By its moral commitment to long-term wealth creation and commitment to the interests of others, stewardship adopts the virtuous and responsible leadership obligations essential to earning high trust and a commitment to excellence[242]. Although TE is an extremely high ethical standard for leaders,

---

[240] *Ibid*, p. 5.

[241] *Ibid*, p. 20.

[242] Caldwell, C., Hayes, L., Karri, R., and Bernal, P., 2008. "Ethical Stewardship: The Role of Leadership Behavior and Perceived Trustworthiness." *Journal of Business Ethics*, Vol. 78, Iss. 1/2, pp. 153-164.

stewardship matches that same high standard and demonstrates to followers that their leader pursues ethical ideals that honor the leader's responsibilities to others.

FIVE VIRTUES OF STEWARDSHIP

As stewards interact with those whom they lead and serve, their actions reflect their morality and virtuousness. In particular, stewards demonstrate five virtues that distinguish them from other would-be leaders that typically lack these same qualities.

Humility

Humility contributes the capacity to appreciate one's potential greatness and the greatness of others while simultaneously acknowledging the moral obligation to fulfill that potential, coupled with the desire to also help others to achieve their best possible version of themselves.

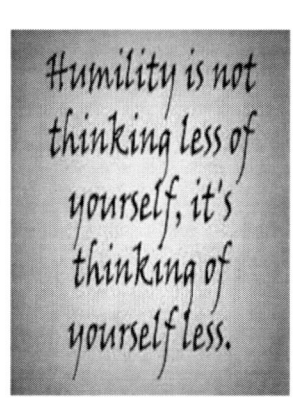

The three pillars of humility are 1) a proper understanding of oneself, 2) a deep appreciation of the value of others, and 3 commitment to constantly be learning and improving motivated by a desire to serve others better[243]. Humble stewards readily take personal responsibility when organizational

---

[243] For insights into the importance of these three pillars, see Owens, B. P. & Hekman, D. R., (2016). "How Does Leader Humility Influence Team Performance? Exploring the Mechanisms of Contagion and Collective Promotion Focus." *Academy of Management Journal*, Vol. 59, Iss. 3, pp. 1088-1111.

performance is below standard but give credit to others when outstanding results are achieved[244]. Humility contributes the capacity to appreciate one's potential greatness and the greatness of others while simultaneously acknowledging the moral obligation to fulfill that potential, coupled with the desire to also help others to achieve their best possible version of themselves[245].

Perseverance

Perseverance is the capacity to devote oneself to accomplishing the best that one is capable of achieving[246]. Driven by a recognition of the potential of self and others, stewards demonstrate the fierce commitment and resolve that typifies the greatest leaders[247]. Perseverance is willing to endure disappointment, delay, and difficulties without giving up and steadfastly maintains a dedication to achieving excellence and a dogged pursuit of worthy goals[248].

Perseverance is willing to endure disappointment, delay, and difficulties without giving up and steadfastly maintains a dedication to achieving excellence and a dogged pursuit of worthy goals.

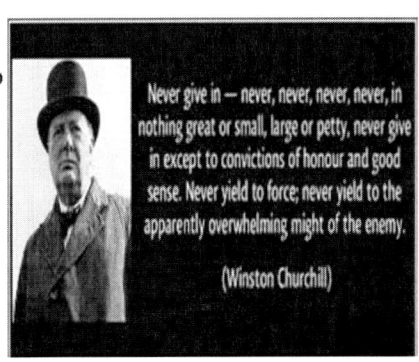

Never give in — never, never, never, never, in nothing great or small, large or petty, never give in except to convictions of honour and good sense. Never yield to force; never yield to the apparently overwhelming might of the enemy.

(Winston Churchill)

---

[244] These great qualities of humility are described by Collins, J., (2001). *Good to Great: Why Some Companies Make the Leap . . . And Others Don't*. New York: HarperCollins.

[245] This inspiring quality of enlightened leaders is described throughout Anderson, V. and Caldwell, C. (Eds.). (2018). *Humility as Enlightened Leadership*. Hauppage, New York: NOVA Publishing.

[246] See Duckworth, A., (2018). *GRIT: The Power of Passion and Perseverance*. New York: Scribner.

[247] The importance of this fierce resolve is addressed in Collins, J., (2001), *op. cit.*

[248] Duckworth, A., (2018)., *op. cit.*

Passion

Stewards are driven by an inner fire[249]. Their realization that greatness is possible motivates them to view that greatness as a moral obligation that they are compelled to pursue[250]. Inspired by their ability to envision what is possible, stewards willingly embrace their responsibility to serve others and to dedicate themselves to honoring their highest potential[251]. Their passion to achieve great goals rises to the level of a covenantal duty and a sacred obligation which enables them to fulfill what they accept as their personal identity[252].

> Inspired by their ability to envision what is possible, stewards willingly embrace their responsibility to serve others and to dedicate themselves to honoring their highest potential. Their passion to achieve great goals rises to the level of a covenantal duty and a sacred obligation which enables them to fulfill what they accept as their personal identity.

Perspective

Stewards possess a vision that others rarely grasp[253]. This perspective affirms that constant improvement is essential for success and that good is never good enough[254]. The capacity to envision what is ultimately possible

---

[249] *Ibid.*

[250] Caldwell, C., (2018). "Humility as a Divine Gift" in Anderson, V. and Caldwell, C. (Eds.). (2018). *Humility as Enlightened Leadership.* Hauppage, New York: NOVA Publishing.

[251] *Ibid.*

[252] Fulfilling this personal identity is a driving force identified as a key element of passion in Duckworth, A., (2018), *op. cit.* and is recognized as a sacred responsibility and covenantal duty in DePree, M., (2004). *Leadership is an Art.* New York: Crown Publishing.

[253] The ability to share this vision is cited as a critical component to leadership success in Kouzes, J. M. & Posner, B. Z., (2017). *The Leadership Challenge: How to Make Extraordinary Things Happen in Organizations.* San Francisco, CA: Jossey-Bass.

[254] Collins, J., (2001), *op. cit.*

and to communicate that vision to others enables stewards to encourage those with whom they work and to assist them in the tasks required to accomplish great goals[255].

The capacity to envision what is ultimately possible and to communicate that vision to others enables stewards to encourage those with whom they work and to assist them in the tasks required to accomplish great goals.

Character

Stewards possess the personal integrity to honor who they truly are and their responsibility to treat others so well that others also recognize their potential and strive to achieve it.

Despite the challenges facing them and those with whom they work, stewards willingly accept the responsibility to pursue opportunities and

---

[255] Kouzes, J. M. & Posner, B. Z., (2017), *op. cit.*

confront the obstacles that must be overcome to succeed[256]. Stewards possess the personal integrity to honor who they truly are and their responsibility to treat others so well that others also recognize their potential and strive to achieve it[257].

As stewards incorporate these five virtues into their lives and in their relationships with others, their personal example is easily recognized and inspires others to adopt these same virtues[258].

CONCLUSION

Great leaders, as Cameron noted, are rare[259]. As leaders accept responsibility and accountability for their organizations, as they demonstrate virtuousness in their relationships and in honoring their obligations, they enhance their ability to earn the trust and followership of others and motivate others to become their best[260]. Leaders who are ethical stewards need not be perfect and free of faults. No one is. Nonetheless, stewards distinguish themselves from others by their commitment to constantly improve and to help others to succeed in the journey to accomplish worthy goals.

The challenge for individuals who are not yet stewards is to examine what they want to accomplish in their lives and to discover within themselves the great unlocked potential that each one of us possesses[261]. Although fulfilling one's highest potential is certainly no easy task, within the heart of hearts of every man and woman is the knowledge that (s)he can do more and has the potential to make a truly meaningful contribution in the lives of others[262]. As individuals respond to that inner voice to become their

---

[256] The integrity of leaders and their responsibility to assist others to succeed is addressed in Deming, W. E., (2000). *Out of the Crisis*. Cambridge, MA: MIT Press.

[257] These profound qualities associated with understanding one's identity and the greatness in others is an important theme of Covey, S. R., (2004), *op. cit.*

[258] See, for example, Owens, B. P. & Hekman, D. R., (2016), *op. cit.*

[259] Cameron begins his article with this observation. See Cameron, K., (2011), *op. cit.*, p. 25.

[260] Covey, S. R., (2004), *op. cit.*

[261] *Ibid.*

[262] Abraham Maslow confirms this inner drive to self-actualize as the highest motivating force in all men and women in Maslow, A. H., (2014). *Toward a Psychology of Being*. Floyd, VA: Sublime Publications.

best, they discover the importance of becoming stewards and fulfill their own highest potential[263].

The challenge for individuals who are not yet stewards is to examine what they want to accomplish in their lives and to discover within themselves the great unlocked potential that each one of us possesses.

REFERENCES

Anderson, V. and Caldwell, C. (Eds.). (2018). *Humility as Enlightened Leadership*. Hauppauge, New York: Nova Science Publishing.

Block, P., (2013). *Stewardship: Choosing Service Over Self-Interest*. San Francisco, CA: Jossey-Bass. Cameron, K., (2011). "Responsible Leadership as Virtuous Leadership." *Journal of Business Ethics*, Vol. 98, pp. 25-35.

Caldwell, C., and Anderson, V. "Transformative Ethics: An Integrative Model of Ethical Stewardship." A working draft of a paper presented at the *International Academy of Management and Business Conference* in New Orleans, Louisiana on January 20, 2017.

Caldwell, C., (2018). "Humility as a Divine Gift" in Anderson, V. and Caldwell, C. (Eds.). (2018). *Humility as Enlightened Leadership*. Hauppauge, New York: Nova Science Publishing.

Caldwell, C., Hayes, L., Karri, R., and Bernal, P., 2008. "Ethical Stewardship: The Role of Leadership Behavior and Perceived

---

[263] *Ibid.*

Trustworthiness." *Journal of Business Ethics*, Vol. 78, Iss. 1/2, pp. 153-164.

Collins, J., (2001). *Good to Great: Why Some Companies Make the Leap . . . and Others Don't*. New York: Harper Collins.

Covey, S. R., (2004). *The 8th Habit: From Effectiveness to Greatness*. New York: Free Press, pp. 98-99.

Deming, W. E., (2000). *Out of the Crisis*. Cambridge, MA: MIT Press.

DePree, M., (2004). *Leadership is an Art*. New York: Crown Publishing.

Duckworth, A., (2018). *GRIT: The Power of Passion and Perseverance*. New York: Scribner.

Gert, B. & Gert, J. (2017) "The Definition of Morality." In *The Stanford Encyclopedia of Philosophy*, Edward N. Zalta (ed.), and found online on October 18, 2018 at https://plato.stanford.edu/archives/fall2017/entries/morality-definition/>.

Gilligan, C., (2016). In a Different Voice: Psychological Theory and Women's Development. Boston, MA: *Harvard University Press*.

Hernandez, M., (2008). "Promoting Stewardship Behavior in Organizations." Journal of Business Ethics, Vol. 80, Iss. 1, pp. 121-128, Hernandez, M., (2012). "Toward an Understanding of the Psychology of Stewardship." *Academy of Management Review*, Vol. 37, Iss. 2, pp. 172-193.

Howard, T., (2018). *"Carol Gilligan Theory: How Women Develop Their Sense of Self."* Betterhelp found online on October 19, 2018 at https://www.betterhelp.com/advice/psychologists/carol-gilligan-theory-how-women-develop-their-sense-of-self/.

Kouzes, J. M. & Posner, B. Z., (2017). *The Leadership Challenge: How to Make Extraordinary Things Happen in Organizations*. San Francisco, CA: Jossey-Bass.

Maslow, A. H., (2014). *Toward a Psychology of Being*. Floyd, VA: Sublime Publications.

Owens, B. P. & Hekman, D. R., (2016). "How Does Leader Humility Influence Team Performance? Exploring the Mechanisms of Contagion and Collective Promotion Focus." *Academy of Management Journal*, Vol. 59, Iss. 3, pp. 1088-1111.

Pava, M., (2003). *Leading with Meaning: Using Covenantal Leadership to Build a Better Organization*. New York: St. Martin's Press.

Zizek, B., Garz, D. & Nowak, E., (Eds.), (2015*). Kohlberg Revisited*. Rotterdam, The Netherlands: Sense Publications.

Chapter 8

TRANSFORMATIVE LEADERSHIP – PRACTICAL APPLICATIONS AND IMPLICATIONS FOR TRUST

Despite the need for organizations to be able to separate themselves from their competitors through the unique contributions of their employees[264], the overwhelming majority of employees are looking actively for new jobs and feel neither fully engaged nor deeply committed to the organizations for which they work. According to a recent study reported in the *Washington Post*, "the vast majority of 17,000 U.S. workers in 19 industries who participated in a survey conducted by the nonprofit group Mental Health America and the Faas Foundation said they are unhappy with their jobs[265]." According to the study, "71 percent also said that they are looking to change employers[266]."

[264] The unique contribution of employees in generating a competitive advantage is identified in Pfeffer, J., (1998). *The Human Equation: Building Profits by Putting People First*. Boston, MA: Harvard Business Review Press and Beer, M., (2009). *High Commitment High Performance: How to Build a Resilient Organization for Sustained Advantage*. San Francisco, CA: Jossey-Bass.

[265] This report was cited by Marks, G., (2017). "Study: 71 Percent of Employees are Looking for New Jobs." *Washington Post*, October 19, 2017 found online on November 2, 2018 at https://www.washingtonpost.com/news/on-small-business/wp/2017/10/19/study-71-percent-of-employees-are-looking-for-new-jobs/?utm_term=.162c6ce61b20.

[266] *Ibid.*

According to a recent study reported in the **Washington Post**, "the vast majority of 17,000 U.S. workers in 19 industries who participated in a survey conducted by the nonprofit group Mental Health America and the Faas Foundation said they are unhappy with their jobs."

The failure of organizations to earn the trust and followership of employees has reached epic proportions in an arms-length world where the employment-at-will doctrine undermines any promise of employer good faith and 40% of all jobs are now part-time, temporary, or contract positions[267]. The unfortunate reality is that trust in leaders has declined in virtually all areas of the public and private sector, according to a study reported in the *Harvard Business Review*[268]. The failure of leaders to earn the commitment and trust of followers has been a root cause of ineffective organizations for eight decades[269] and reflects the inability of leaders to demonstrate that they are worthy of the commitment, dedication, and extra-mile effort required for successful performance in today's modern organization[270].

---

[267] See Caldwell, C. and Anderson, V., (2017). *Strategic Human Resource Management.* Hauppage, NY: NOVA Publications and Caldwell, C., Atwijuka, S. & Okpala, C. O., (2018). "Compassionate Leadership in an Arms-Length World." Working paper currently under review in the *International Journal of Business and Management.*

[268] Harrington, M., (2017). "Study: People's Trust has Declined in Business, Media, Government, and NGOs." *Harvard Business Review.* January 16, 2017, found online on November 2, 2017 at https://hbr.org/2017/01/survey-peoples-trust-has-declined-in-business-media-government-and-ngos

[269] The ineffectiveness of leaders was a major issue addressed by Chester Barnard in 1938 in a series of lectures presented at Harvard College and recorded in Barnard, C. I., (1938). *The Functions of the Executive.* Cambridge, MA: Harvard College.

[270] See Caldwell, C., and Ndalamba, K. K., (2017). "Trust and Being 'Worthy' – The Keys to Creating Wealth." *Journal of Management Development,* Vol. 36, Iss. 8, pp. 1076-1086 and Christensen, C. M., (2016). *The Innovator's Dilemma: When New Technologies Cause Great Firms to Fail.* Boston, MA: Harvard Business Review Press.

The failure of leaders to earn the commitment and trust of followers has been a root cause of ineffective organizations for eight decades and reflects the inability of leaders to demonstrate that they are worthy of the commitment, dedication, and extra-mile effort required for successful performance in today's modern organization.

In response to the ineffectiveness of so many organizations, a new "Transformative Leadership" (TL) model of ethical leadership has been developed that addresses the obligations of leaders to employees throughout an organization and that integrates key elements of six other highly-respected leadership perspectives[271]. The purposes of this chapter are to both describe this new TL model and identify its practical advantages in earning the trust and followership of today's employees. The chapter begins with a summary of TL and the six leadership perspectives upon which it is based. Following that explanation, we then identify twelve trust-related qualities of TL that clarify how leaders who adopt that leadership model can increase the commitment of those with whom they work. We conclude the chapter with a brief summary.

UNDERSTANDING TRANSFORMATIVE LEADERSHIP

When TL was introduced into the leadership literature, it was described as "an ethically-based leadership model that integrates a commitment to values and outcomes by optimizing the long-term interests of stakeholders and society and honoring the moral duties owed by organizations to their

---

[271] This Transformative Leadership model was developed in Caldwell, C., (2012). Moral Leadership: A Transformative Model for Tomorrow's Leaders. New York: Business Expert Press and described in Caldwell, C., Dixon, R. D., Floyd, L., Chaudoin, J., Post., J., and Cheokas, G. (2012). "Transformative Leadership: Achieving Unparalleled Excellence." *Journal of Business Ethics*, Vol 109, Iss. 2, pp. 175-187.

stakeholders[272]." The "transformative" label for this model had its roots in leadership scholars, Warren Bennis and Burt Nanus, who called for a higher standard of transformative leader "who commits people to action, who converts followers into leaders, and who may convert leaders into agents of change[273]." TL focuses on action, adapting to change, creating supportive relationships, and honoring duties owed to others.

Transformative Leadership

"An ethically-based leadership model that integrates a commitment to values and outcomes by optimizing the long-term interests of stakeholders and society and honoring the moral duties owed by organizations to their stakeholders."

The strength of TL is that it is a virtuous framework for treating others that is based upon insights from six highly-regarded leadership perspectives.

The strength of TL is that it is a virtuous framework for treating others that is based upon insights from six highly-regarded leadership perspectives. Those six leadership perspectives are shown in Figure 1 and each of the perspectives is briefly summarized below.

---

[272] This definition is found at Caldwell, C., *et al.*, (2012), *op. cit.*, p. 123.

[273] See Bennis, W. G. & Nanus, B., (2007). *Leaders: Strategies for Taking Charge*. New York: HarperCollins, p. 16.

Figure 1. Contributing leadership perspectives and transformative leadership.

Transformational Leadership

Transformational Leadership is a powerful leadership perspective that seeks to achieve both the growth and development of individual employees and the accomplishment of high priority organizational goals as firms deal with the ever-present forces of change[274]. A primary focus of Transformational Leadership is its emphasis on engaging with employees. Burns recognized the potential for excellence that is achievable by emphasizing "power with" rather than "power over" others in the pursuit of priorities that enhanced the capabilities of employees[275].

Transformational leadership is grounded in a duty-based moral foundation and is made up of four components[276].

---

[274] The work of James MacGregor Burns is seminal in the discussion of Transformational Leadership. See Burns, J. M., (2010). *Leadership*. New York: Harper Perennial.

[275] The wisdom of "power with" others was identified by the brilliant Mary Parker Follett two generations before Burns advocated that same idea. See Graham, P., (2003). *Mary Parker Follett: Prophet of Management*. Frederick, MY: Beard Books.

[276] For a summary of these four key elements, see Bass, B. M., & Steidlmeier, P., (1999). "Ethics, Character, and Authentic Transformational Leadership Behavior". *Leadership Quarterly*, Vol. 10, pp. 181–218. See also Riggio, R. E., (2014). "Four Elements of Transformational Leader.' *Psychology Today*, November 15, 2014 found online on November 3, 2018 at https://www.psychologytoday.com/us/blog/cutting-edge-leadership/201411/the-4-elements-transformational-leaders.

Idealized Influence – Leaders become positive role models who influence others by their personal examples and consistency in following the values they espouse.

Inspirational Motivation – Leaders motivate and inspire others to become their best selves and to achieve shared goals.

Intellectual Stimulation – Leaders challenge others to be creative and innovative in adding their personal contribution to the organization's pursuit of excellence.

Individualized Consideration – By demonstrating genuine concern for the individual needs of followers, leaders acknowledge and support each person's highest potential.

These four components enable followers to raise the bar of their own personal development while contributing to the performance of the organization[277]. By pursuing excellence, empowering others to become their best, seeking the best interests of both the individual and the organization, and exemplifying what they communicate to others, Transformational Leaders honor their obligations to their colleagues and their firms[278].

> The commitment of Transformational Leaders in pursuing outcomes that benefit all stakeholders reflects the synergistic nature of Transformational Leadership. This commitment to constant improvement and synergy enables individuals and organizations to add value and achieve better outcomes.

The commitment of Transformational Leaders in pursuing outcomes that benefit all stakeholders reflects the synergistic nature of Transformational Leadership. This commitment to constant improvement and synergy enables individuals and organizations to add value and achieve

---

[277] Caldwell, C., et al., (2012), *op. cit.*
[278] *Ibid.*

better outcomes. The Transformational Leader's commitment to excellence earns the high trust of employees and enables companies to respond to opportunities that arise in a constantly evolving world[279].

Charismatic Leadership

Charismatic Leaders are advocates of what they believe to be a highly moral purpose that may rise to the level of a ''calling[280].''. The noble vision of Charismatic Leadership inspires others to join the crusade and redefines the identity and purpose of followers. Charismatic leaders articulate a compelling vision and inspire high levels of personal commitment which creates energy and dedication that enables followers to go the extra mile in the pursuit of a noble objective[281].

Charismatic leaders articulate a compelling vision and inspire high levels of personal commitment which creates energy and dedication that enables followers to go the extra mile in the pursuit of a noble objective

The ability of Charismatic Leaders to create personal connection and to exemplify moral principles encourages others to examine their lives, fulfill a higher potential, and adopt a virtue-based ethical standard[282]. That focus

[279] See Caldwell, C., (2015). "Six Insights for Transformative Leaders." *Graziadio Business Review* published by Pepperdine University and available online at http://gbr.pepperdine.edu/tag/transformative-leaders.

[280] Lussier, R. N., & Achua, C. F. (2009). *Leadership: Theory, Application, and Skill Development* (4th ed.). Mason, OH: South-Western, pp. 334-338.

[281] Lussier, R. N., & Achua, C. F. (2009), *op. cit.*

[282] This point about the Charismatic Leader is identified in Caldwell, C., Truong, D., Linh, P., & Tuan, A. (2011). "Strategic Human Resource Management as Ethical Stewardship." *Journal of Business Ethics*, Vol. 98, No. 1, pp, 171–182.

centers on striving to honor core principles and pursuing noble objectives and generates "energy, passion, and excitement" within an organization[283]. Charismatic Leadership inspires rising aspirations that transcend personal accomplishments in the pursuit of a high ideal and a better world[284].

The great Martin Luther King comes to mind when we think of Charismatic Leaders. King possessed the personal capacity to relate to people, to inspire them in the pursuit of a noble goal, and the mantle of dedicated personal commitment that enabled him to emulate this leadership perspective[285]. King's skill as a communicator, his ability to persuade, and his capacity to reach others at the emotional level typify the qualities most commonly associated with this leadership perspective and explain how the Charismatic Leader creates the personal connection with followers that inspires personal commitment and trust.

Covenantal Leadership

Covenantal Leadership views the leader's obligation to followers and to the organization as a truly sacred responsibility that transcends simply being an example to others[286]. The Covenantal Leader has the responsibility to truly empower others, to provide them with his or her own insights and wisdom, and to guide and instruct others in the pursuit of new meanings and new truth. Implicit within Covenantal Leadership is the belief that people's lives are interconnected and that the leader's responsibilities extend to the larger society and contain a broad array of moral responsibilities.

---

[283] See Senge, P. M., (2006). *The Fifth Discipline; The Art & Practice of the Learning Organization.* New York: Doubleday.

[284] See Conger, J. A. & Kanungo, R. N., (1998). *Charismatic Leadership in Organizations.* Thousand Oaks, CA: Sage Publications.

[285] For examples of King's ability to inspire and give hope, see King, M. J. & Washington, J. M., (2003). *A Testament of Hope. The Essential Writings and Speeches.* New York: HarperCollins.

[286] Covenantal Leadership was development by Moses Pava as a leadership perspective. See Pava, M., (2003). *Leading with Meaning: Using Covenantal Leadership to Build a Better Organization.* New York: St. Martin's Press.

The Covenantal Leader is a teacher who shares insights and imparts the wisdom of his or her experiences. The Covenantal Leader is constantly in search of new truths and the search for new truth is part of the leader's legacy to others[287]. Openness to truth and the ability of a leader to avoid dependence upon past assumptions enhance the leader's ability to manage change without being tied to old paradigms[288]. Covenantal leaders create learning cultures that share information, provide others with opportunities to experiment, and constantly strive to help others to improve[289].

The Covenantal Leader is constantly in search of new truths and the search for new truth is part of the leader's legacy to others  **DISCOVER TRUTH**

Creating an organization that is constantly learning and that makes truth its priority enables that organization to be capable of evolving with the demands of change. Covenantal Leaders honor the moral obligation to not only discover the truth but to share it with others in the pursuit of their best interests. Their commitment to the truth, their personal integrity, and their dedication to others' welfare earns these leaders the trust, respect, and followership of others[290].

---

[287] Caldwell, C., and Hasan, Z. 2016, "The Covenantal Leader – Honoring Implicit Relationships with Employees." *Graziadio Business Review*, Vol. 19, Iss. 2 and available online at http://gbr.pepperdine.edu/2016/10/the-covenantal-leader.
[288] Caldwell, C., et al., (2012), *op. cit.*
[289] *Ibid*. See also Senge, P. M., (2006), *op. cit.*
[290] Pava, M., (2003), *op. cit.*

Principle-Centered Leadership

Principle-Centered Leadership is based upon the belief that there are universally-accepted "correct principles and values" that guide individuals in organizations as they strive to be effective and as they maintain relationships with others[291]. In addition, it is a values-based foundation for governing oneself and honoring relationships with others that defines leadership as an ethical obligation to honor duties owed to others[292]. Principle-centered leadership combines a pursuit of high ideals for becoming a better person with an obligation to create a more productive and moral society[293].

> Moral leadership behavior encompasses a set of moral duties to 1) add value today, 2) to do no harm, and 3) to contribute to the welfare of individuals and society in the future.

Moral leadership behavior encompasses a set of moral duties to 1) add value today, 2) to do no harm, and 3) to contribute to the welfare of individuals and society in the future[294]. The obligation of the Principle-Centered Leader is to apply correct principles and adhere to those principles in governing one's dealings with others[295]. Principle-centered leadership incorporates an Aristotelian or virtue-based ethical foundation based upon

---

[291] Principle-Centered Leadership was popularized as a leadership perspective by Stephen R. Covey. See Covey, S. R., (1992). *Principle-Centered Leadership*. New York: Fireside Press.

[292] *Ibid.*

[293] *Ibid.*

[294] Lennick, D. & Kiel, F., (2015). *Moral Intelligence 2.0: Enhancing Business Performance and Leadership Success in Turbulent Times*. Boston, MA: Pearson Education.

[295] Covey, S. R., (204). *The 8th Habit: From Effectiveness to Greatness*. New York: Free Press.

those principles and promotes the flourishing of both individuals and organizations[296].

Principle-Centered Leadership begins "from the inside-out" and asks leaders to live by and to apply correct principles and values in their lives. By honoring these principles and values, Principle-Centered Leaders commit themselves to a virtuous standard of responsible management and strive to be accountable and responsible leaders[297]. These leaders build trust by their commitment to others' flourishing and their personal integrity in honoring correct principles[298].

Level 5 Leaders

Level 5 Leadership is a leadership perspective developed by Jim Collins in his research about companies that have made the successful transition from being good to becoming truly great[299]. Level 5 Leaders combine a fierce resolve or stoic determination to achieve organization success with a profound humility[300]. Level 5 Leaders are not self-serving but willingly take personal responsibility for the shortcomings of their organizations while giving other team members the credit for outstanding results[301].

Level 5 Leaders recognize that success is not their own and stress the importance of hiring great people. They make bringing excellent people into the organization the heart of their organization strategy. They are passionate and driven to achieve organizational successes and are deeply committed to developing people within their organizations as well. However, Collins found that Level 5 Leaders avoided taking a high profile within their organizations and were often understated leaders who willingly gave others

---

[296] Caldwell, C., et al., (2012), *op. cit.*
[297] This correlation between virtuous leadership and responsible leadership is explained in Cameron, K., (2011). "Responsible Leadership as Virtuous Leadership." *Journal of Business Ethics*, Vol. 98, pp. 25-35.
[298] *Ibid.*
[299] See Collins, J., (2001). *Good to Great: Why Some Companies Make the Leap. and Others Don't.* New York: HarperCollins.
[300] *Ibid.*
[301] *Ibid.*

the credit for achievements[302]. Their ethical focus emphasized the obligation of leaders to achieve the best possible organization results[303].

Level 5 Leaders recognize that success is not their own and stress the importance of hiring great people. They make bringing excellent people into the organization the heart of their organization strategy.

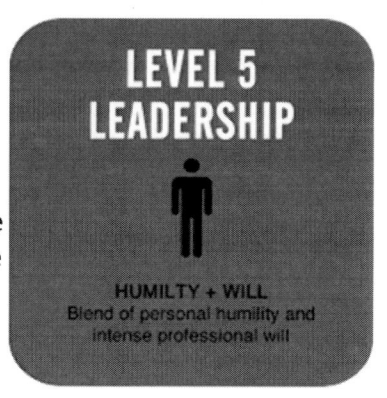

Collins described these leaders as "looking into the mirror" when mistakes occurred and accepting personal responsibility but "looking out the window" and fully acknowledging the important roles of others when organizations achieved their goals.

The Yin and Yang of Level 5 Leadership

The focus and example of Level 5 Leaders earns others' respect and trust. Level 5 Leadership is not about high-profile leadership but those who work with those leaders recognize both their contribution to the success of the organization and their commitment to the organization's achievements. Collins described these leaders as "looking into the mirror" when mistakes occurred and accepting personal responsibility but "looking out the window" and fully acknowledging the important roles of others when organizations achieved their goals[304].

---

[302] *Ibid.*
[303] Caldwell, et al., (2012), *op. cit.*
[304] Collins, J., (2001), *op. cit.*

Servant Leadership

Servant Leaders are acknowledged to be leaders focused on a philosophy of leadership that enriches the lives of individuals, creates great organizations, and seeks to create a better world[305]. The underlying theme of servant leadership is that the leader pursues the needs, desires, interests, and welfare of others above personal self-interest[306]. As a steward committed to helping others, the servant leader honors duties owed to individuals, the organization, and to society[307].

The underlying theme of servant leadership is that the leader pursues the needs, desires, interests, and welfare of others above personal self-interest. As a steward committed to helping others, the servant leader honors duties owed to individuals, the organization, and to society.

"We rise by lifting others."

-Robert Ingersoll

Servant leaders willingly accept the responsibility to "define reality" within an organization and use that defining responsibility to focus on the obligations owed to others[308]. The responsibility of the leader to "be a servant first" is the underlying assumption of Servant Leadership and is viewed as a sacred obligation with profound ramifications[309]. Servant

---

[305] This definition comes from the Robert K. Greenleaf Center for Servant Leadership website found on November 3, 2018 at https://www.greenleaf.org/what-is-servant-leadership/,

[306] Block, P., (2013). *Stewardship: Choosing Service Over Self-Interest*. San Francisco, CA: Jossey-Bass.

[307] See Greenleaf, R. K. & Spears, L. C., (2002). *Servant Leadership: A Journey Into Legitimate Power & Greatness 25th Anniversary Edition*. New York: Paulist Press.

[308] This obligation to define reality is the first responsibility of the leader, according to DePree, M., (2004). *Leadership is an Art*. New York: Crown Publishing, p. 11.

[309] Greenleaf, R. K. & Spears, L. C., (2002), *op. cit.*

Leaders seek "the good of those being led and those whom the organization serves[310]."

The commitment of Servant Leaders to serving others, coupled by the behaviors that demonstrate that obligation to others' welfare, earns them the trust of those whom they serve. The underlying assumption of Servant Leadership is that this honoring of the leader's obligation to serve others reflects the authentic desire of the selfless.

Although there may be overlap in these six leadership perspectives, each perspective also makes a significant ethical contribution that strengthens the ability to merit stakeholder trust. The evidence suggests that today's leaders persist in following leadership practices that are actually detrimental to creating high trust and that are in conflict with their long-term best interests.

These six leadership perspectives which make up TL share common qualities in their commitment to excellence, their recognition of the importance of seeking both optimal organizational performance and individual growth, and their passion in honoring values owed to others. Although there may be overlap in these six leadership perspectives, each perspective also makes a significant ethical contribution to TL that strengthens its ability to merit stakeholder trust. The evidence suggests that today's leaders persist in following leadership practices that are actually detrimental to creating high trust and that are in conflict with their long-term best interests.

---

[310] This quote comes from Hamilton, F., & Nord, W. R. (2005). "Book Review of *Practicing Servant-leadership: Succeeding through Trust, Bravery, and Forgiveness.*" *Academy of Management Review*, Vol. 30, Iss. 4, pp. 875–877.

Transformative Leadership and Building Trust

Leaders who have adopted the ethical perspectives of TL have recognized that the qualities that they possess are a powerful contributor to building the high commitment and trust that are conditions precedent to creating great organizations. In this section we identify twelve qualities of TL that enable it to generate follower trust.

Integrating the Financial and the Social

TLs recognize the importance of both the financial priorities of business and its social obligations to society[311]. Leaders that honor both responsibilities demonstrate a contextual sensitivity to a troubled world[312].

Addressing Long-Term and Short-Term Priorities

Recognizing that value creation must take place at both the short-term and the long-term levels, TLs balance those objectives in honoring moral duties[313].

Honoring Principles and Values

Principles are recognized guidelines for decision-making but TLs understand that both principles and values must be considered[314]. In making decisions, values often must supersede guiding principles.

---

[311] Paine, L. S., (2002). *Value Shift: Why Companies Must Merge Financial and Social Imperatives to Achieve Superior Performance*. Boston, MA: McGraw-Hill Education.

[312] Anderson, V., Ndalamba, K. K., and Caldwell, C., (2017). "Social Responsibility in a Troubled World: A Virtuous Perspective." *International Journal of Public Leadership*, Vol, 13, Iss. 2, pp 98-115.

[313] Lennick, D. & Kiel, F., (2015), *op. cit.*

[314] Covey, S. R., (2004), *op. cit.*

Principles are recognized guidelines for decision-making but leaders understand that both principles and values must be considered. In making decisions, values often must supersede guiding principles.

Understanding Opportunities and Risks

Great leaders thoughtfully evaluate risks and carefully consider how they should be evaluated[315]. Risk-taking and opportunities are closely associated but need not jeopardize an organization's future[316].

Serving Present and Future Stakeholders

The needs of future stakeholders must be considered as moral consequences when making economic decisions. Short-term profit-taking must also be weighed against the impact of decisions on long-term wealth creation.

---

[315] See Collins, J. & Hansen, M. T., (2011). *Great by Choice: Uncertainty, Chaos, and Luck – Why Some Thrive Despite Them All*. New York: HarperBusiness.
[316] *Ibid.*

The needs of future stakeholders must be considered as moral consequences when making economic decisions[317]. Short-term profit-taking must also be weighed against the impact of decisions on long-term wealth creation[318].

Modeling Patience and Persistence

Effective leaders recognize that the timing of decisions is often a critical issue is achieving a desired outcome[319]. TLs demonstrate the ability to be patient in making decisions that are optimally effective, but they are also driven and dedicated to achieving the best possible organizational results.

Merging the Noble and the Practical

Great leaders understand the importance of defining reality in evaluating what is possible[320]. At the same time, TLs view that which they are striving to accomplish as both a covenantal duty and a sacred obligation[321].

Combining Character and Competence

In the pursuit of excellence, TLs strive to act with integrity in honoring commitments and in serving others. They recognize that character without competence is nonetheless ineffective as well[322].

---

[317] See Hosmer, L. T., (2010). *The Ethics of Management* (7th ed.). Boston, MA: McGraw-Hill Education.

[318] Pfeffer, J., (1998), *op. cit.*

[319] Caldwell, C. & Anderson, V., (2017). *Competitive Advantage: Strategies, Management, and Performance*. Hauppage, NY: NOVA Publications.

[320] DePree, M., (2004), *op. cit.*

[321] Pava, M., (2003), *op. cit.*

[322] Covey, S. R., (1992), *op. cit.*

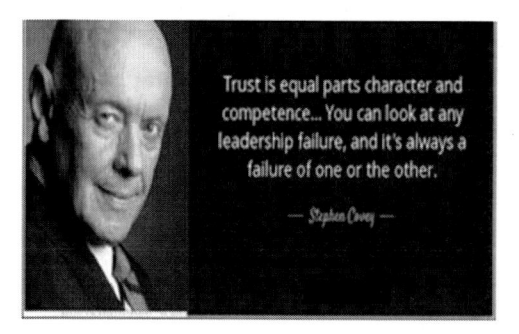

In the pursuit of excellence, leaders strive to act with integrity in honoring commitments and in serving others. They recognize that character without competence is nonetheless ineffective as well.

Demonstrating Flexibility and Consistency

Adapting to change is an essential reality facing every leader and every organization[323]. Flexibility and consistency are both important factors, with consistency requiring a commitment to a company's fundamental values[324].

Balancing Accountability and Compassion

Leaders must hold themselves and their organizations accountable to high standards if they are going to achieve success[325]. TLs willingly accept personal accountability for their organization's failures. At the same time, compassionate leaders are deeply committed to helping their colleagues succeed and support them in their efforts[326].

Recognizing Limits and Possibilities

Truly effective leaders strive to surpass previous achievements and are dedicated to the pursuit of optimal performance that far exceeds industry

[323] Burns, J. M., (2010), *op. cit.*
[324] Collins, J. & Porras, J, I., (2004). *Built to Last: Successful Habits of Visionary Companies.* New York: Harper Business.
[325] Collins, J., (2001), *op. cit.*
[326] Caldwell, C., Atwijuka, S. & Okpala, C. O., (2018), *op. cit.*

standards[327]. At the same time, they make wise and well-considered decisions when evaluating new opportunities[328].

> Truly effective leaders strive to surpass previous achievements and are dedicated to the pursuit of optimal performance that far exceeds industry standards. At the same time, they make wise and well considered decisions in evaluating opportunities.

Serving the Individual and the Organization

TLs exemplify a balanced commitment to the needs of individual organization members and view that responsibility as a debt owed to those individuals, rather than simply as a quid pro quo obligation[329]. These leaders believe that honoring relationships to employees and treating them as valued partners earns their commitment and results in organization success[330].

> Transformative Leaders not only incorporate the highest standards of the six perspectives that make up this leadership model but honor the obligation of individuals and organizations to add value and create wealth that not only generates profits but that makes a better world.

---

[327] Collins, J., (2001), *op. cit.*

[328] Collins, J. & Hansen, M. T., (2011), *op. cit.*

[329] See DePree, M., (2004), *op. cit.* and Burns, J. M., (2010), *op. cit.*

[330] *Ibid.* See also Block, P., (2013), *op. cit.*

Each of these important qualities goes a long way in earning TLs the high trust that enables them to achieve follower commitment and loyalty that seems to have evaporated in many organizations. By demonstrating these abilities, TLs not only incorporate the highest standards of the six perspectives that make up this leadership model but honor the obligation of individuals and organizations to add value and create wealth that not only generates profits but that makes a better world.

CONCLUSION

The assumptions upon which many past leaders have based success have proven to be unsuccessful, yet leaders have persisted in resisting changes in their mental paradigms despite decades of evidence that they are going down the wrong path. Only when practitioners and scholars open their minds to a new paradigm of thinking about duties owed to others will individuals and organizations be willing to change their behaviors and adopt more ethically-based leadership values.

> Only when practitioners and scholars open their minds to a new paradigm of thinking about duties owed to others will individuals and organizations be willing to change their behaviors and adopt more ethically-based leadership values.

Today's organization leaders face challenges that demand that leaders manage change to compete successfully in a world where organization leaders have come under increased criticism and lost the trust of the public and their own employees. TL addresses the needs of the modern organization by (1) emphasizing the need for long-term wealth creation, (2)

focusing on the achievement of both normative and instrumental priorities, and (3) demonstrating that leaders have examined both who they are and the duties that leaders owe to others. Understanding the nature of the foundational elements of TL provides powerful insights for those who seek to lead as well as those who study leadership.

REFERENCES

Anderson, V., Ndalamba, K. K., and Caldwell, C., (2017). "Social Responsibility in a Troubled World: A Virtuous Perspective." *International Journal of Public Leadership*, Vol, 13, Iss. 2, pp 98-115.

Barnard, C. I., (1938). *The Functions of the Executive*. Cambridge, MA: Harvard College.

Bass, B. M., & Steidlmeier, P., (1999). "Ethics, Character, and Authentic Transformational Leadership Behavior". *Leadership Quarterly*, Vol. 10, pp. 181–218.

Beer, M., (2009). *High Commitment High Performance: How to Build a Resilient Organization for Sustained Advantage*. San Francisco, CA: Jossey-Bass.

Bennis, W. G. & Nanus, B., (2007). *Leaders: Strategies for Taking Charge*. New York: Harper Collins, p. 16.

Block, P., (2013). *Stewardship: Choosing Service Over Self-Interest*. San Francisco, CA: Jossey-Bass.

Burns, J. M., (2010). *Leadership*. New York: Harper Perennial.

Caldwell, C., Atwijuka, S. & Okpala, C. O., (2018). "Compassionate Leadership in an Arms-Length World." Working paper currently under review in the *International Journal of Business and Management*.

Caldwell, C. & Anderson, V., (2017). *Competitive Advantage: Strategies, Management, and Performance*. Hauppauge, NY: Nova Science Publishers.

Caldwell, C. and Anderson, V., (2017). *Strategic Human Resource Management*. Hauppauge, NY: Nova Science Publishers

Caldwell, C., and Ndalamba, K. K., (2017). "Trust and Being 'Worthy' – The Keys to Creating Wealth." *Journal of Management Development*, Vol. 36, Iss. 8, pp. 1076-1086

Caldwell, C., and Hasan, Z. 2016, "The Covenantal Leader – Honoring Implicit Relationships with Employees." *Graziadio Business Review*, Vol. 19, Iss. 2 and available online at http://gbr.pepperdine.edu/ 2016/10/the-covenantal-leader.

Caldwell, C., (2015). "Six Insights for Transformative Leaders." *Graziadio Business Review* published by Pepperdine University and available online at http://gbr.pepperdine.edu/tag/transformative-leaders.

Caldwell, C., (2012). *Moral Leadership: A Transformative Model for Tomorrow's Leaders*. New York: Business Expert Press

Caldwell, C., Dixon, R. D., Floyd, L., Chaudoin, J., Post., J., and Cheokas, G. (2012). "Transformative Leadership: Achieving Unparalleled Excellence." *Journal of Business Ethics*, Vol 109, Iss. 2, pp. 175-187.

Caldwell, C., Truong, D., Linh, P., & Tuan, A. (2011). "Strategic Human Resource Management as Ethical Stewardship." *Journal of Business Ethics*, Vol. 98, No. 1, pp, 171–182.

Cameron, K., (2011). "Responsible Leadership as Virtuous Leadership." *Journal of Business Ethics*, Vol. 98, pp. 25-35.

Christensen, C. M., (2016). *The Innovator's Dilemma: When New Technologies Cause Great Firms to Fail*. Boston, MA: Harvard Business Review Press.

Collins, J. & Hansen, M. T., (2011). *Great by Choice: Uncertainty, Chaos, and Luck – Why Some Thrive Despite Them All*. New York: Harper Business.

Collins, J. & Porras, J, I., (2004). *Built to Last: Successful Habits of Visionary Companies*. New York: Harper Business.

Collins, J., (2001). *Good to Great: Why Some Companies Make the Leap. and Others Don't*. New York: HarperCollins.

Conger, J. A. & Kanungo, R. N., (1998). *Charismatic Leadership in Organizations*. Thousand Oaks, CA: Sage Publications.

Covey, S. R., (2004). *The 8th Habit: From Effectiveness to Greatness*. New York: Free Press.

Covey, S. R., (1992). *Principle-Centered Leadership*. New York: Fireside Press.

DePree, M., (2004). *Leadership is an Art*. New York: Crown Publishing, p. 11.

Graham, P., (2003). *Mary Parker Follett: Prophet of Management*. Frederick, MY: Beard Books.

Greenleaf, R. K. & Spears, L. C., (2002). *Servant Leadership: A Journey Into Legitimate Power & Greatness 25th Anniversary Edition*. New York: Paulist Press.

Hamilton, F., & Nord, W. R. (2005). "Book Review of *Practicing Servant-leadership: Succeeding through Trust, Bravery, and Forgiveness*." *Academy of Management Review*, Vol. 30, Iss. 4, pp. 875–877.

Harrington, M., (2017). "Study: People's Trust has Declined in Business, Media, Government, and NGOs." *Harvard Business Review*. January 16, 2017, found online on November 2, 2017 at https://hbr.org/2017/01/survey-peoples-trust-has-declined-in-business-media-government-and-ngos

Hosmer, L. T., (2010). *The Ethics of Management* (7th ed.). Boston, MA: McGraw-Hill Education.

King, M. J. & Washington, J. M., (2003). *A Testament of Hope. The Essential Writings and Speeches*. New York: HarperCollins.

Lennick, D. & Kiel, F., (2015). *Moral Intelligence 2.0: Enhancing Business Performance and Leadership Success in Turbulent Times*. Boston, MA: Pearson Education.

Lussier, R. N., & Achua, C. F. (2009). *Leadership: Theory, Application, and Skill Development* (4th ed.). Mason, OH: South-Western, pp. 334-338.

Marks, G., (2017). "Study: 71 Percent of Employees are Looking for New Jobs." *Washington Post*, October 19, 2017 found online on November 2, 2018 at https://www.washingtonpost.com/news/on-small-business/wp/2017/10/19/study-71-percent-of-employees-are-looking-for-new-jobs/?utm_term=.162c6ce61b20.

Paine, L. S., (2002). *Value Shift: Why Companies Must Merge Financial and Social Imperatives to Achieve Superior Performance*. Boston, MA: McGraw-Hill Education.

Pava, M., (2003). *Leading with Meaning: Using Covenantal Leadership to Build a Better Organization.* New York: St. Martin's Press.

Pfeffer, J., (1998). The Human Equation: Building Profits by Putting People First. Boston, MA: *Harvard Business Review* Press

Riggio, R. E., (2014). "Four Elements of Transformational Leader.' *Psychology Today*, November 15, 2014 found online on November 3, 2018 at https://www.psychologytoday.com/us/blog/cutting-edge-leadership/201411/the-4-elements-transformational-leaders.

Robert K. *Greenleaf Center for Servant Leadership* website found on November 3, 2018 at https://www.greenleaf.org/what-is-servant-leadership/.

Senge, P. M., (2006). *The Fifth Discipline; The Art & Practice of the Learning Organization.* New York: Doubleday.

Chapter 9

SELF-ASSESSMENT AND THE STEWARDSHIP ROLE – WHAT LEADERS OFTEN LACK

In the thousands of books and hundreds of thousands of articles that have been written about leadership, scholars and would-be experts offer their opinions about a multitude of activities, qualities, behaviors, and antecedents of great leadership. The many who have written about the subject provide counsel about what leadership is and isn't, whether it is an in-born or developed quality, and the moral and ethical obligations of those who aspire to lead. Despite all that has been written about leadership, there remains enthusiastic disagreement about many elements of leadership, the role of leaders in human relations, and the building of effective organizations.

The challenge of this book transcends much of what has been proposed about leaders and leadership, adopting a focus on stewardship rather than simply on leadership. We have defined stewardship as an elite level of interpersonal relationships, suggesting that stewards have a higher degree of moral obligation than is attributed to most leaders. We have described stewardship as both a covenantal obligation and a noble calling wherein the steward seeks the optimal best interests of all who (s)he serves in the pursuit of long-term value creation. The standards of stewardship, we propose, demand a far greater understanding of the nature of oneself, one's relationships, and one's sense of personal identity than most leaders have thought to develop.

The focus of this chapter is on recognizing the importance of self-assessment as a critical determining factor that enables an individual to become a steward rather than simply a leader. The chapter premise is that stewardship's commitment to a higher capacity to serve others is due to that person's understanding of herself or himself by integrating important elements of self-assessment. We begin the chapter by briefly framing the importance of the self-assessment process and explaining the concept of the identity standard as a model for one's identity and personal self-assessment. After describing that model, we then identify ten distinct elements of self-assessment that distinguish the leader from the steward. We conclude this chapter with a challenge to those who seek to become great leaders to adopt this higher level of self-assessment to become stewards in today's challenging world.

THE IMPORTANCE OF SELF-ASSESSMENT

The process of self-assessment in evaluating is a complex calculus[331] typically occurring at the unconscious and subconscious levels that we use to control our behavior to comply with whom we believe we are[332]. Discovering oneself requires a clear vision of one's strengths, weaknesses, beliefs, expectations, and responsibilities. In Plato's *Apology*, Socrates declared at his trial defense, "The unexamined life is not worth living[333]" and affirmed the importance of conducting that self-examination. Self-assessment requires a humble willingness to look honestly at oneself,

---

[331] This phrasing about the subtle calculus used in behavioral choices comes from Creed, W. E. D. & Miles, R. E., (1996). "Trust in Organizations: A Conceptual Framework Linking Organizational Forms, Managerial Philosophies, and the Opportunity Costs of Controls" in R. M. Kramer and T. R. Tyler (Eds.), *Trust in Organizations: Frontiers of Theory and Research*. Thousand Oaks, CA: Sage Publications, pp. 16–38.

[332] Burke, P. J. & Stets, J. E., (2009). *Identity Theory*. Oxford, UK: Oxford University Press.

[333] This quote attributed to Socrates is found in Plato, (2017). *Apology*. Seattle, WA: Create Space Independent Publishing.

motivated out of a genuine desire to fulfill one's highest potential and to serve others[334].

Self-assessment demands an understanding of one's personal identity and the standards to which one holds herself or himself. One's identity includes those fundamental elements that are central, enduring, and distinctive about a person[335]. Each person's identity is constantly evolving but often at the subconscious and unconscious levels. For each individual, their identity standard or comparator is the basis for their self-image[336]. This identity standard or encompasses the personal perceptions about how a person expects that (s)he should relate to others and to the world. Figure 1 summarizes the process by which individuals examine themselves and their conduct at both the conscious and subconscious levels[337].

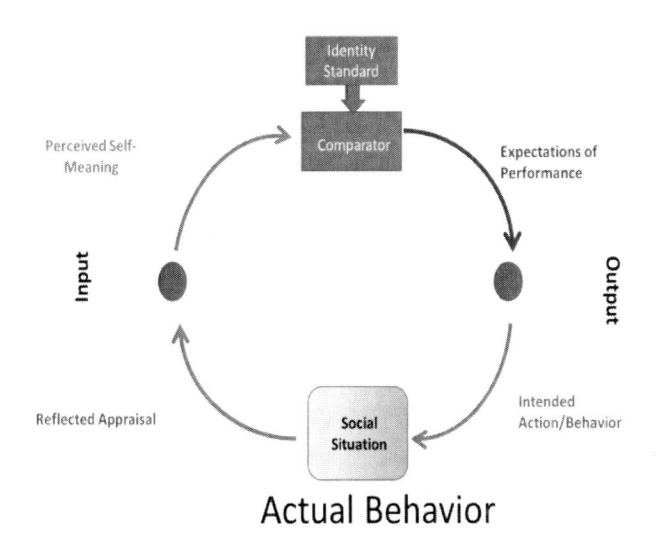

Figure 1. Identity Standard and Comparator.

[334] The importance of this honest assessment is described in Anderson, V. & Caldwell, C., (2018). *Humility as Enlightened Leadership*. Hauppage, NY: NOVA Publishing and Covey, S. R., (2004). *The 8th Habit: From Effectiveness to Greatness*. New York: Free Press.

[335] See Caldwell, C. (2009). "Identity, Self-Deception, and Self-Awareness: Ethical Implications for Leaders and Organizations." *Journal of Business Ethics*, Vol. 90, Supp. 3, pp. 393-406.

[336] This identity standard or comparator is described in Burke, P. J. & Stets, J. E., (2009), *op. cit.*

[337] Fishbein, M. & Ajzen, I. (2015). *Predicting and Changing Behavior: The Reasoned Action Approach*. New York: Psychology Press.

The identity standard identifies the basis for one's expected actions which are then translated into intended behaviors. The social situation in which a person is engaged creates the context in which a person then acts. Those actions generate a reflected appraisal from others and compared to the original standard. That reflected appraisal results in a positive or negative perception about how a person acted with its accompanying self-meaning. Failure to meet the original identity standard may result in an affirmation of that standard or the desire to change one's future performance as the identity standard is again used to define expectations about one's identity and future performance[338].

The constant but typically unconscious assessment of personal behavior affects one's perceptions about his/her identity. However, conscious awareness of how we see ourselves is often elusive and may result in ongoing rationalization, self-justification, cognitive dissonance, fundamental attribution error, and denial about who we are, how we view ourselves, and what constitutes our standards for our own behaviors[339]. Our ability to conduct an effective self-assessment is seriously reduced by the degree to which we are able to understand at the conscious level the respective elements of our identity standard and our behavioral choices.

DISTINGUISHING ELEMENTS OF SELF-AWARENESS

As individuals apply the principles of self-assessment in their lives, they increase their capacity to be effective leaders. Great leaders who rise to the level of stewards are distinguished from less effective leaders in large measure because of the difference in the way that stewards apply ten elements of self-assessment. The purpose of this section is to identify ten of the elements of self-assessment that stewards excel in that enable them to be exponentially more effective than others in serving organizations and the stakeholders in them.

---

[338] In Burke, P. J. & Stets, J. E., (2009), *op. cit.*

[339] The Arbinger Institute, (2018). *Leadership and Self-Deception: Getting Out of the Box.* San Francisco, CA: Berrett-Kohler Publishing.

Self-Examination – The willingness and desire to understand who one truly is and to realize one's highest potential enables individuals to closely examine what is important, what they do well, what they love to do, and what their conscience affirms that they do[340]. Leaders who are high in humility engage in this self-examination process in the quest to have "a correct understanding of oneself[341]." Stewards willingly engage in this process as they seek to fulfill their identities and honor their moral responsibilities[342].

Self-Awareness – One's conscious knowledge about the nuances of who we are and how we relate to other people is the foundation of self-awareness[343]. As a fundamental element of emotional and social intelligence,[344] self-awareness also includes our ability to identify how we are perceived by others and how we incorporate those perceptions into our own identity[345]. Self-awareness has been identified as a critical skillset to keeping an organization aligned and is a distinguishing quality of great leadership[346]. Stewards demonstrate self-awareness by understanding the needs of others and by focusing on meeting others' needs[347].

Self-Sacrifice – Self-sacrifice and selflessness are actions in which a person puts others' interests ahead of their own, typically to achieve a superordinate goal[348]. The willingness to pursue the larger interests of others

---

[340] This discovery of who one really is has been described as "finding your voice" in Covey, S. R., (2004). *The 8th Habit: From Effectiveness to Greatness.* New York: Free Press.

[341] The self-examination process of leaders and its relationship to humility is addressed in Caldwell, C., Ichiko, R., and Anderson, V., 2017. "Understanding Level 5 Leaders -- The Ethical Perspective of Leadership Humility." *Journal of Management Development,* Vol. 36, Iss. 5, pp. 724-732.

[342] The importance of self-examination in stewardship is addressed in Caldwell, C., Hayes, L., Karri, R., and Bernal, P., 2008. "Ethical Stewardship: The Role of Leadership Behavior and Perceived Trustworthiness." *Journal of Business Ethics,* Vol. 78, Iss. 1/2, pp. 153-164.

[343] Caldwell, C., (2009), *op. cit.*

[344] See, for example Goleman, D., (2005). *Emotional Intelligence: Why It Can Matter More than IQ.* New York: Bantam Books.

[345] Caldwell, C., (2009), *op. cit.*

[346] See Hougaard, R., Carter, J., & Afton, M., (2018). "Self-Awareness Can Help Leaders More Than an MBA Can." *Harvard Business Review Digital Articles,* January 1, 2018, pp. 2-5.

[347] Caldwell, C., Bischoff, S. J., and Karri, R. 2002. "The Four Umpires: A Paradigm for Ethical Leadership," *Journal of Business Ethics,* Vol. 36, Iss. 1/2, pp. 153-163.

[348] The notion of leadership as a calling is addressed as a fundamental element of charismatic leaders. See Conger, J. A. & Kanungo, R. N., (1998). *Charismatic Leadership in Organizations.* Thousand Oaks, CA: Sage Publications.

Cam Caldwell and Verl Anderson

demonstrates a leader's commitment to both normative and instrumental values[349]. Putting service to others over personal self-interest is a defining quality of stewardship[350] and demonstrates the steward's focus on values and priorities that earn her/him the respect of others[351].

Self-Regard – An individual's self-regard is the measure to which that person views her or his self as worthy of self-respect and esteem. A person holds herself or himself in high self-regard when personal actions demonstrate character and integrity – as would be the case if a person is satisfied that how (s)he has acted is consistent with an identity standard[352]. Stewards typically have a high self-regard because they possess the humility to understand not only the worth of others but their own worth as well[353].

Self-Discovery – In the process of self-discovery, individuals obtain a clearer understanding of their own identities, especially with regard to how they view their moral or spiritual selves. Self-discovery is directly connected with Spiritual Intelligence and one's choices associate with conscience[354]. This transcendent capability, though rare, empowers a steward to devote herself or himself to a purpose and mission that ennobles the individual and that seeks to benefit others[355].

Self-Control – Self-control is the ability to discipline one's motives, impulses, and behaviors to achieve a specific result[356]. Martialing our ability to control our responses in accord with our core beliefs is a lifelong

[349] See Caldwell, C., Hayes, L., Karri, R., and Bernal, P., 2008. "Ethical Stewardship: The Role of Leadership Behavior and Perceived Trustworthiness." *Journal of Business Ethics*, Vol. 78, Iss. 1/2, pp. 153-164 and Hernandez, M., (2012). "Toward an Understanding of the Psychology of Stewardship." *Academy of Management Review*, Vol. 37, Iss. 2, pp. 172-193.

[350] Block, P., (2013). *Stewardship: Choosing Service Over Self-Interest*. San Francisco, CA: Jossey-Bass.

[351] Van Knippenberg, B. & van Knippernberg, D., (2005). "Leader Self-Sacrifice and Leadership Effectiveness: The Moderating Role of Leader Prototypicality." *Journal of Applied Psychology*, Vol. 90, Iss. 1, pp. 25-37.

[352] Burke, P. J. & Stets, J. E., (2009), *op. cit.*

[353] Anderson, V. & Caldwell, C., (2018), *op. cit.*

[354] Covey, S. R. (2004), *op. cit.*

[355] This quality and its contribution to others is identified in Okpala, C. O. & Caldwell, C. (2019). "Humility, Forgiveness, and Love: The Heart of Ethical Stewardship." Paper accepted for publication in the *Journal of Values-Based Leadership* in Summer 2019.

[356] Covey, S. R. (2004), *op. cit.*

challenge[357]. The capacity of a leader to recognize what is needed to manage her or his actions and responses is the most important part of self-control[358]. Self-control demands insight and integrity. The ability to govern responses and to act appropriately to help others to succeed is a critical skill set of emotional intelligence and enables a steward to interact with others in a manner that serves both the individual and the organization[359].

Self-Deception – Self-deception is the denial or rationalization that important information is not relevant in opposing a logical position that one believes. It involves holding two conflicting ideas in mind at the same time without acknowledging the conflict[360]. Self-deception is extremely common and often involves personal denial about oneself and one's character. Because stewards are committed to self-examination and self-understanding, they are far less likely than others to engage in self-deception[361].

Self-Mastery – The ability to not only control one's responses but to develop high levels of personal competence is the essence of self-mastery. One's capacity to achieve self-mastery demands a unique commitment, focus, and discipline that comes from a desire to fulfill a noble purpose. Self-mastery typically is the result of a devoted effort over an extended period of time to acquire a virtue or capability[362]. Stewards increase their likelihood to achieve self-mastery because of their commitment to who they are and what they seek to accomplish.

Self-Actualization – Recognizing and achieving the best version of oneself provides the capacity for the personal transformation that enables individuals to reach higher than they have previously believed was possible[363]. This achievement of one's highest potential is considered to be

---

[357] Tarvis, C. & Aronson, E. (2015). *Mistakes Were Made (but Not by Me): Why We Justify Foolish Beliefs, Bade Decisions and Hurtful Acts*. New York: Houghton Mifflin.

[358] *Ibid.*

[359] Goleman, D., (2005), *op. cit.*

[360] Caldwell, C., (2009)., *op. cit.*

[361] Anderson, V. & Caldwell, C., (2018), *op. cit.*

[362] Taylor, C. S., (2017). *The Journey: A Self-Mastery Workbook*. Seattle, WA: Create Space Independent Publishing.

[363] *Ibid.*

a basic need of every person[364]. Stewards develop the level of commitment that increases their ability to achieve outcomes that others rarely achieve[365].

Self-Fulfillment – The ability to achieve what one has dreamed of accomplishing in life is the essence of self-fulfillment[366]. For stewards, the achievement of one's dreams transcends self-interest and commonly includes outcomes and results that benefit others[367]. It is in honoring this commitment to duties outside of themselves that stewards fulfill the criteria of their identity standard[368].

All ten of these self-related qualities that are associated with self-assessment may be possessed by leaders but are much more likely to be present in ethical stewards who are much more likely to be committed to the standards of excellence that are the foundation of the stewardship philosophy[369].

REFERENCES

Anderson, V. & Caldwell, C., (2018). *Humility as Enlightened Leadership.* Hauppauge, New York: Nova Science Publishing.

Arbinger Institute, (2018). *Leadership and Self-Deception: Getting Out of the Box.* San Francisco, CA: Berrett-Kohler Publishing.

Archer, M. S., (2001). *Being Human: The Problem of Agency.* New York: Cambridge University Press.

Beer, M., (2009). *High Commitment High Performance: How to Build a Resilient Organization for Sustained Advantage.* San Francisco, CA: Jossey-Bass.

---

[364] Maslow, A. H., (2014). *Toward a Psychology of Being.* Plano, TX: Sublime Books.

[365] Okpala, C. O. & Caldwell, C. (2019). "Humility, Forgiveness, and Love: The Heart of Ethical Stewardship." Paper accepted for publication in the *Journal of Values-Based Leadership* in Summer 2019.

[366] Gewirth, A., (2009). *Self-Fulfillment.* Princeton, NJ: Princeton University Press.

[367] Block, P., (2013). *Stewardship: Choosing Service Over Self-Interest.* San Francsco, CA: Jossey-Bass.

[368] Compare both Burke, P. J. & Stets, J. E., (2009), *op. cit* and Anderson, V. & Caldwell, C., (2018), *op. cit.*

[369] Hernandez, M., (2012), *op. cit.*

Block, P., (2013). *Stewardship: Choosing Service Over Self-Interest*. San Francisco, CA: Jossey-Bass.

Block, P., (2013) and Barnard, C. I., (1938). *The Functions of the Executive*. Cambridge, MA: Harvard College.

Burke, P. J. & Stets, J. E., (2009). *Identity Theory*. Oxford, UK: Oxford University Press

Caldwell, C. 2018. *Leadership, Ethics, and Trust*. Newcastle upon Tyne, UK: Cambridge Scholars Publishing.

Caldwell, C. & Anderson, V., (2017*). Competitive Advantage: Strategies, Management, and Performance*. Hauppauge, New York: Nova Science Publishing.

Caldwell, C., Ichiko, R., and Anderson, V., 2017. "Understanding Level 5 Leaders -- The Ethical Perspective of Leadership Humility." *Journal of Management Development,* Vol. 36, Iss. 5, pp. 724-732.

Caldwell, C., Hayes, L., Karri, R., and Bernal, P., (2008), *op. cit.* and Hernandez, M., (2012). "Toward an Understanding of the Psychology of Stewardship." *Academy of Management Review*, Vol. 37, Iss. 2, pp. 172-193.

Caldwell, C. (2009). "Identity, Self-Deception, and Self-Awareness: Ethical Implications for Leaders and Organizations." *Journal of Business Ethics*, Vol. 90, Supp. 3, pp. 393-406.

Caldwell, C., Hayes, L., Karri, R., and Bernal, P., (2008). "Ethical Stewardship: The Role of Leadership Behavior and Perceived Trustworthiness." *Journal of Business Ethics*, Vol. 78, Iss. 1/2, pp. 153-164.

Caldwell, C., Bischoff, S. J., and Karri, R. (2002). "The Four Umpires: A Paradigm for Ethical Leadership," *Journal of Business Ethics*, Vol. 36, Iss. 1/2, pp. 153-163.

Christensen, C. M., (2016). *The Innovator's Dilemma: When New Technologies Cause Great Firms to Fail*. Boston, MA: Harvard Business Review Press.

Collins, J. & Porras, J. I., (2004). *Built to Last: Successful Habits of Visionary Companies*. New York: Harper Business.

Conger, J. A. & Kanungo, R. N., (1998). *Charismatic Leadership in Organizations*. Thousand Oaks, CA: Sage Publications.

Covey, S. R., (2004). *The 8ᵗʰ Habit: From Effectiveness to Greatness*. New York: Free Press.

Creed, W. E. D. & Miles, R. E., (1996). "Trust in Organizations: A Conceptual

Deming. W. E., (2000). *Out of the Crisis*. Cambridge, MA: MIT Press.

Framework Linking Organizational Forms, Managerial Philosophies, and the Opportunity Costs of Controls" in R. M. Kramer and T. R. Tyler (Eds.), *Trust in Organizations: Frontiers of Theory and Research*. Thousand Oaks, CA: Sage Publications, pp. 16–38.

Fishbein, M. & Ajzen, I. (2015). *Predicting and Changing Behavior: The Reasoned Action Approach*. New York: Psychology Press.

Gewirth, A., (2009). *Self-Fulfillment*. Princeton, NJ: Princeton University Press.

Goleman, D., (2005). *Emotional Intelligence: Why It Can Matter More than IQ*. New York: Bantam Books.

Hougaard, R., Carter, J., & Afton, M., (2018). "Self-Awareness Can Help Leaders More Than an MBA Can." *Harvard Business Review Digital Articles*, January 1, 2018, pp. 2-5.

McGregor, J. M., (2010). *Leadership*. New York: Harper Perennial Modern Classics.

Maslow, A. H., (2014). *Toward a Psychology of Being*. Plano, TX: Sublime Books.

Okpala, C. O. & Caldwell, C. (2019). "Humility, Forgiveness, and Love: The Heart of Ethical Stewardship." Paper accepted for publication in the *Journal of Values-Based Leadership* in Summer 2019.

Pfeffer, J., (1998). The Human Equation: Building Profits by Putting People First. Boston, MA: *Harvard Business Review* Press.

Plato, (2017). *Apology*. Seattle, WA: Create Space Independent Publishing.

Simon, H. A., (1997). *Administrative Behavior* (4ᵗʰ ed.). New York: Free Press.

Tarvis, C. & Aronson, E. (2015). *Mistakes Were Made (but Not by Me): Why We Justify Foolish Beliefs, Bade Decisions and Hurtful Acts*. New York: Houghton Mifflin.

Taylor, C. S., (2017*). The Journey: A Self-Mastery Workbook*. Seattle, WA: Create Space Independent Publishing.

Van Knippenberg, B. & van Knippernberg, D., (2005). "Leader Self-Sacrifice and Leadership Effectiveness: The Moderating Role of Leader Prototypicality." *Journal of Applied Psychology*, Vol. 90, Iss. 1, pp. 25-37.

Chapter 10

STEWARDSHIP AND PERSONAL LEARNING – RAISING THE BAR

As leaders seek to enhance their effectiveness and to raise the bar of their personal standards, they become more like ethical stewards and increase their capacity to earn the trust of others[370]. The distinguishing qualities between leadership and stewardship include the clarity in which stewards see themselves, their wisdom in defining relationships with others, and in the application of those insights in guiding their personal conduct.

The focus of this chapter is on the nature of the learning process which leaders incorporate as they develop the skills of ethical stewardship. The chapter begins by describing the process of learning that we all engage in as explained by the Theory of Reasoned Action. After identifying the nature of that universal learning process, we identify and describe in depth the five refined virtues that enable leaders to evolve into ethical stewards. Each of these qualities is explained in terms of its ability to provide a leader with increased understanding of the moral obligations of the ethical steward and the capacity to apply that knowledge. The chapter then identifies the process

---

[370] This insight is emphasized in Caldwell, C., Hayes, L., Karri, R., and Bernal, P., (2008). "Ethical Stewardship: The Role of Leadership Behavior and Perceived Trustworthiness." *Journal of Business Ethics*, Vol. 78, Iss. 1/2, pp. 153-164.

that leaders can follow to incorporate these five virtues of ethical stewardship into their own leadership relationships.

The distinguishing qualities between leadership and stewardship include the clarity in which stewards see themselves, their wisdom in defining relationships with others, and in the application of those insights in guiding their personal conduct.

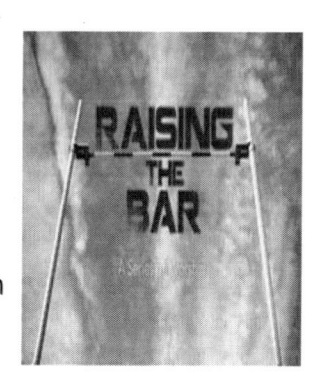

LEARNING AND THE THEORY OF REASONED ACTION

The process of learning is a complex calculus in which learners observe or experience the world around them in acquiring information which they seek to apply in their own lives. Learning can occur at multiple levels and involves a sorting process whereby individuals interpret information, build hypotheses about its application, and test those hypotheses in their interactions with the world in which they live.

The process of learning is a complex calculus in which learners observe or experience the world around them in acquiring information which they seek to apply in their own lives.

The Nobel Laureate, Herbert Simon, explained that learning involved the filtering of information and the eliminating of uncertainty in an effort to improve decision-making, increase predictability, and control future conditions[371]. The importance of learning in organizations[372] has been defined as a distinguishing quality that determines whether a firm will succeed or fail and establishing a learning culture in an organization is often regarded as a condition precedent to sustainability and competitive advantage[373].

In its complexity, the process of learning has been described as consisting of four elements[374]. The four elements of cognitive beliefs, affective attitudes, conative intentions, and applied behaviors are integrated into a Theory of Reasoned Action (TRA) which explains how individual behaviors are decided and acted upon[375] and how people learn[376]. Figure 1 identifies the four elements which make up the framework of TRA.

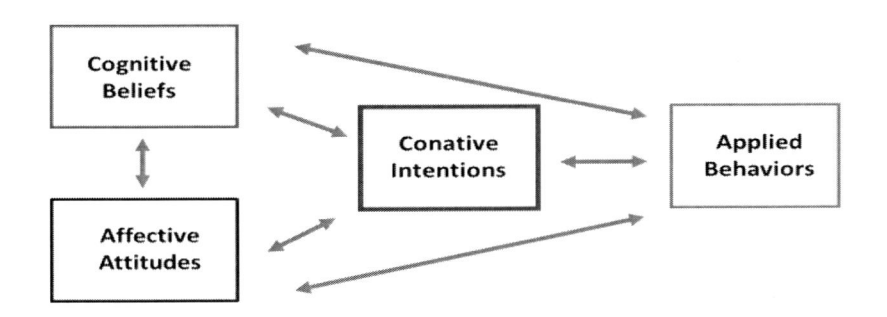

Figure 1. Learning and the Theory of Reasoned Action.

---

[371] See Simon, H. A., (1997). *Administrative Behavior* (4th ed.). New York: Free Press.

[372] See Senge, P. M., (2006). *The Fifth Discipline: The Art & Practice of the Learning Organization.* New York: Random House.

[373] Christensen, C. M., (2016). *The Innovator's Dilemma: When New Technologies Cause Great Firms to Fail.* Boston, MA: Harvard Business Review Press.

[374] Glasper, K. & Caldwell, C., (2016). "Teaching Through 'Transforming Learning,' an Integrative Model for Business and Public Administration Education." *Business and Management Research,* Vol. 5, No. 1, pp. 19-28 and available online at http://www.sciedupress.com/journal/index.php/bmr/article/view/9088/5495.

[375] Fishbein, M. & Ajzen, I., (2015). *Predicting and Changing Behavior: The Reasoned Action Approach.* New York: Psychology Press.

[376] Glasper, K. & Caldwell, C., (2016), *op. cit.*

Conative beliefs are learned as people obtain an understanding of key principles, terms, facts, concepts, and definitions associated with learning about a topic[377]. Cognitive beliefs have been the foundation of the learning process for many years and involve a hierarchical set of increasingly complex levels of understanding about ideas and information[378]. Affective attitudes are associated with emotions and feelings associated with the learning process and includes such factors as how one feels about oneself and others, how a person learns, and the values that influence actions and decisions[379]. Conative intentions encompass the process by which a person reaches a threshold of understanding about ideas – including the decision to "unlearn" what one previous thought (s)he believed by testing assumptions about which one intends to act upon[380]. Applied behaviors involve the learning-by-doing process, including both successes and failures, and may include testing the practical application of ideas to determine their relevance[381].

Individuals constantly gather, filter, and evaluate information and interpret its significance. At the cognitive level, stewards seek to understand the context in which they are involved with others. In their quest to learn about and understand key issues, stewards strive to keep in mind the purposes for which an organization exists and how resources can best be utilized to accomplish organization goals.

Individuals constantly gather, filter, and evaluate information and interpret its significance. At the cognitive level, stewards seek to understand the context in which they are involved with others. In their quest to learn

---

[377] *Ibid.*

[378] Anderson, L. W. & Krathwohl, D. R., (2000). *A Taxonomy for Learning, Teaching, and Assessing: A Revision of Bloom's Taxonomy of Educational Objectives.* New York: Pearson Publishing.

[379] Glasper, K. & Caldwell, C., (2016), *op. cit.*

[380] *Ibid.*

[381] *Ibid.*

about and understand key issues, stewards strive to keep in mind the purposes for which an organization exists and how resources can best be utilized to accomplish organization goals. Cognitive beliefs include information about both the internal organization and the external environment in which an organization competes[382]. The ability to apply technical information and the understanding of how to apply that information to keep pace with constant change enable organizations to maintain their competitive position[383].

The ability to learn at the affective level enables stewards to not only demonstrate empathy toward others but to engage in supportive actions that touch the lives of those with whom they work.

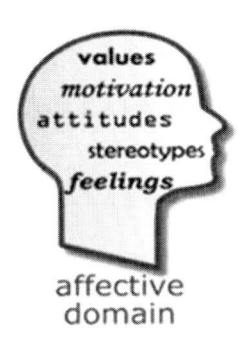

values
motivation
attitudes
stereotypes
feelings

affective domain

The ability to learn at the affective level enables stewards to not only demonstrate empathy toward others but to engage in supportive actions that touch the lives of those with whom they work[384]. As individuals learn more about their own identities and values, they also improve their capacity to relate with others[385]. Great leaders reach out to others, empower and inspire them to become the best version of themselves, and encourage their hearts[386].

---

[382] These two elements of every organization, internal integration and external adaptation, apply to virtually every organizational context. See Schein, E. H. & Schein, P., (2016). Organizational Culture and Leadership (4th ed.). San Francisco, CA: Jossey-Bass.

[383] See Caldwell, C. & Anderson, V., (2017). *Competitive Advantage: Strategies, Management, and Performance.* Hauppage, NY: NOVA Publications.

[384] See Caldwell, C., Atwijuka, S. & Oklpala, C. O., (2018). "Compassionate Leadership in an Arms-Length World." Paper accepted for publication in the *Journal of Business Administration and Management.*

[385] Fink, A. K., & Fink, L. D. (2009). Lessons we Learn from the Voices of Experience. *New Directions for Teaching & Learning,* Vol. 119, pp. 105-113.

[386] These qualities are addressed in Covey, S. R., (2004). The 8th Habit: From Effectiveness to Greatness. New York: Free Press and in Kouzes, J. M. & Posner, B. Z., (2017). *The*

Such leaders constantly refine their interpersonal skills in their efforts to build relationships that demonstrate their concern for others' welfare[387]. Cognitive and affective learning reinforce each other as individuals increase their understanding of themselves and others[388]. This integration of the cognitive and affective learning reinforces personal commitment and affirms values[389].

Learning associated with conative intentions enables individuals to confirm or disconfirm past truths, consolidate learning by testing assumptions about past knowledge, and integrate ethical assumptions into the learning process[390]. The learning process allows individuals to reassess their previously held expectations and perceptions to enhance their ability to evaluate what is and is not valid. Stewards apply this learning process as they evaluate the impact of past assumptions on people's lives, often by developing a more refined understanding of individual needs and the most effective way of achieving optimal outcomes[391].

Learning associated with conative intentions enables individuals to confirm or disconfirm past truths, consolidate learning by testing assumptions about past knowledge, and integrate ethical assumptions into the learning process.

Leadership Challenge: How to Make Extraordinary Things Happen in Organizations (6th ed.). San Francisco, CA: Jossey-Bass.

[387] See Caldwell, C., Hayes, L., and Long, D., (2010). "Leadership, Trustworthiness, and Ethical Stewardship." *Journal of Business Ethics*, Vol. 96, Iss. 4, pp. 497-512.

[388] Fink, L. D., (2003). *Creating Significant Learning Experiences: An Integrated Approach for Designing College Courses.* San Francisco, CA: Jossey-Bass.

[389] *Ibid.*

[390] Glasper, K. & Caldwell, C., (2016), *op. cit.*

[391] See, for example, Caldwell, C., Hayes, L., Karri, R., and Bernal, P., (2008), *op. cit.* and Mezirow, J., (1996). "Toward a Learning Theory of Adult Literacy." *Adult Basic Education*, Vol. 6, No. 3, pp. 115-126.

Ethical stewardship incorporates learning from applied behaviors as a means of both developing skills and affirming the validity of assumptions about correct principles[392]. Stewardship's intention is to pursue outcomes the optimize the creation of value for others and the process of learning by doing provides constant feedback about the interplay of the steward's actions and the responses of others[393]. Learning by doing includes identifying what does not work and can include sharing insights about what is ineffective with others as well. The steward's focus on learning in action enables the learner to differentiate between "good theory" and practical realities.

Learning by doing includes identifying what does not work and can include sharing insights about what is ineffective with others as well. The steward's focus on learning in action enables the learner to differentiate between "good theory" and practical realities.

The ultimate value of TRA is in recognizing that the learning process is ultimately about achieving desired outcomes[394]. The best measure of learning is the degree to which what is learned results in applying behaviors to achieve a valued purpose. Learning provides the opportunity to develop new and better ways to serve others, to create innovative solutions, and to improve the quality of services or products for customers. The integration of the four elements of TRA enables the process of continuous improvement to occur and is entirely consistent with the goals of ethical stewardship[395]. The

---

[392] Fishbein, M. & Ajzen, I., (2015), *op. cit.*
[393] Caldwell, C., Hayes, L., and Long, D., (2010), *op. cit.*
[394] Fishbein, M. & Ajzen, I., (2015), *op. cit.*
[395] Caldwell, C., Hayes, L., and Long, D., (2010), *op. cit.*

quest for constant improvement and the achievement of the best possible long-term result for stakeholders is a defining objective of stewardship[396].

FIVE VIRTUES OF STEWARDSHIP

Although ethical stewards possess many positive qualities, their effectiveness in creating long-term value for organizations and for benefiting the stakeholders of an organization reflect five powerful virtues that differentiate them from many other leaders and which earn them the commitment and trust of followers. Figure 2 is a portrayal of those five virtues which are summarized in this section.

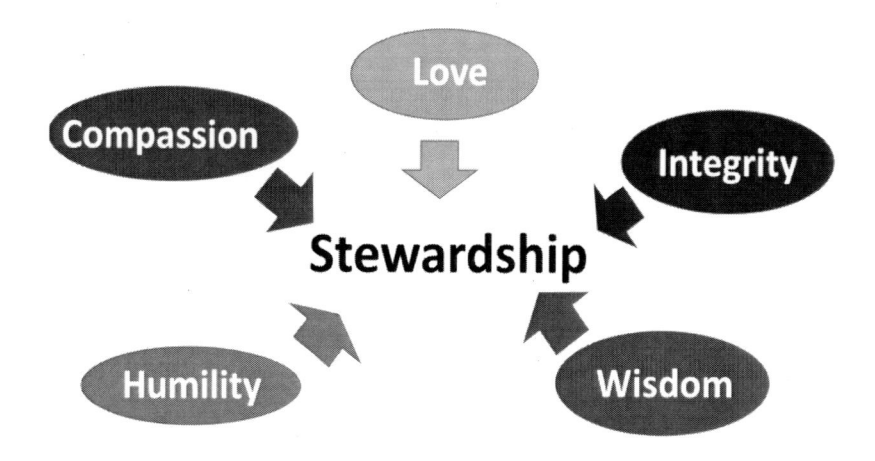

Figure 2. Stewardship's five virtues.

Integrity

Stewardship emphasizes the virtue of integrity and honors relationships with individual stakeholders and with society. Integrity represents both

---

[396] Hernandez, M., (2012). "Toward an Understanding of the Psychology of Stewardship." *Academy of Management Review*, Vol. 37, Iss. 2, pp. 172-193.

honesty and wholeness and the steward personifies both of those qualities[397]. Stewardship honors the obligation to pursue the highest and best in self, in others, and in adding value in the world. Choosing a commitment to service is the foundation of stewardship[398] and stewards also perceive that the opportunity to serve as both a personal calling and a source of individual fulfillment[399].

Stewardship emphasizes the importance of personal integrity in building trust[400]. The supreme quality of leadership is unquestioned integrity and stewards recognize that deception and dishonesty undermine the ability to lead. If great leaders make a mistake, they recognize the importance of taking immediate responsibility for their actions – and if their organization underperforms they similarly accept personal responsibility for its failures[401]. As they learn from personal experience, stewards strive to integrate that learning and to act with integrity in applying new knowledge in the pursuit of excellence.

Integrity demonstrates the steward's appreciation for not only speaking the truth but for acting with a commitment to others' welfare. Integrity demonstrates a loyalty to others and a willingness to assist them to accomplish their goals, rather than seeking to use others simply as a means to accomplishing organizational objectives. Stewards with integrity view others as ends rather than as the means to accomplishing their own agenda. Integrity transcends deception, dishonesty, and half-truths by honoring the truth and being open and honest.

---

[397] For more about integrity and its importance to leaders, see Caldwell, C., (2018). *Leadership, Ethics, and Trust*. Newcastle upon Tyne, UK: Cambridge Scholars Publishing.

[398] Stewardship's commitment to service is clearly the message of Block, P., (2013). *Stewardship: Choosing Service Over Self-Interest*. San Francisco, CA: Jossey-Bass.

[399] The concept of finding self-fulfillment by discovering one's unique significance or voice is the primary message of Covey, S. R., (2004), *op. cit.*

[400] Caldwell, C., Hayes, L., Karri, R., and Bernal, P., (2008), *op. cit.* and Caldwell, C., Hayes, L., and Long, D., (2010), *op. cit.*

[401] This important leadership quality of taking personal responsibility for failures is identified by Collins, J., (2001). *Good to Great: Why Some Companies Make the Leap . . . . And Others Don't*. New York: HarperCollins.

If great leaders make a
mistake, they recognize the
importance of taking
immediate responsibility for
their actions – and if their
organization underperforms
they similarly accept personal
responsibility for its failures.

Compassion

Schopenhauer, the German philosopher, described compassion toward others as the foundation for morality in human interaction[402]. As a leadership quality, compassion includes the ability to understand context and the situation in which others find themselves[403]. Compassion transcends empathy for another person by including an appropriate response that actively assists that other person by relieving their pain or providing help needed to address that person's need[404]. Compassion demonstrates the ability to not only understand others' difficulties but the willingness to serve them by helping them to find solutions for their trials.

Compassion demonstrates
the ability to not only
understand others'
difficulties but the
willingness to serve them
by helping them to find
solutions for their trials.

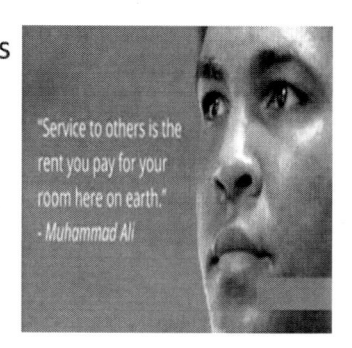

"Service to others is the
rent you pay for your
room here on earth."
- *Muhammad Ali*

---

[402] This insight is found in Schopenhauer, A., (2016). *The Wisdom of Life*. Seattle, WA: Create Space Independent Publishing.
[403] Caldwell, C., Atwijuka, S. & Oklpala, C. O., (2018), *op. cit.*
[404] *Ibid.*

Compassionate leadership is a virtuous response that affirms others' value and purpose and helps others to achieve their goals[405]. Compassion not only inspires others to overcome obstacles but actively assists others to remove the obstacles that burden their lives[406]. By demonstrating genuine compassion, stewards restore in others a sense of hope and bolster their feelings of self-esteem and self-worth[407]. The compassionate leader is a light, not a judge and seeks to "fix the problem" rather than to "fix the blame[408]." At the same time, compassion asks others to be accountable for their own actions and to take responsibility for the decisions made that created their misfortune[409].

As a highly moral standard for interpersonal relationships, compassion incorporates the feminine moral perspective which acknowledges the importance of relationships, responsibility, and caring for others[410]. At the same time, compassion is also focused on masculine moral ideals associated with fairness, utilitarianism, and the rule of law[411] and strives to treat others equitably but with kindness -- despite the mistakes that others may have made that have contributed to their own problems.

Wisdom

Stewards balance knowledge with wisdom. Those who are wise typically have learned from their own mistakes and the errors of others. Confucius explained that a man who has committed a mistake but who does not correct it commits another mistake. Wisdom provides leaders with the vision and clarity to see and understand what others may overlook. Wisdom

---

[405] *Ibid.*

[406] *Ibid.*

[407] *Ibid.*

[408] This advice is found in Price, Q., (2015). *7 Habits of Highly Resilient People: How to Make the Most of Loss, Change and Setbacks*. Seattle, WA: CreateSpace Independent Publishing.

[409] Caldwell, C., Atwijuka, S. & Oklpala, C. O., (2018), *op. cit.*

[410] For a summary of feminine morality, see Gilligan, C., (2016). *In a Different Voice: Psychological Theory and Women's Development*. Boston, MA: Harvard University Press.

[411] The masculine moral perspective is identified in Kohlberg, L., (1981), *The Philosophy of Moral Development: Moral Stages and the Idea of Justice*. New York: Harper & Row.

also includes the ability to understand cause and effect, to predict logical consequences of action, and to anticipate what needs to be done to mitigate a possible problem and prevent a catastrophe.

A man who has committed a mistake and doesn't correct it, is committing another mistake.

- Confucius

The experience and good judgment which wisdom makes possible enables stewards to avoid choices that lead to unnecessary risks and disappointing outcomes. Wisdom includes the practical application of common sense and intelligence in recognizing not only what is likely to occur but to understand the causes of those occurrences. Stewardship incorporates wisdom in the pursuit of that which honors moral obligations to others, pursues both long-term and short-term wealth creation, and avoids doing harm to others[412].

Stewards are wise leaders who recognize that those who lead must first be a servant to others[413]. They understand that great leaders teach others correct principles, define reality, set a personal example, and share the right to make important decisions[414]. Such leaders believe in "power with" rather than "power over" others[415]. Stewards demonstrate wisdom by creating relationships with others that enhance others' abilities and enable those with

---

[412] Wisdom incorporates elements of moral intelligence, as defined in Lennick, D. & Kiel, F., (2015). *Moral Intelligence 2.0: Enhancing Business Performance and Leadership Success in Turbulent Times*. Upper Saddle River, NJ: FT Press.

[413] See Greenleaf, R. K. & Spears, L. C., (2002). *Servant Leadership: A Journey Into Legitimate Power and Greatness 25th Anniversary Edition*. Mahwah, NJ: Paulist Press.

[414] See DePree, M., (2004). *Leadership is an Art*. New York: Crown Publishing.

[415] This concept of "power with" rather than "power over" others was advocated by Mary Parker Follett. See Graham, P., (2003). *Mary Parker Follett: Prophet of Management*. Washington, D.C.: Beard Books.

whom they work to develop their skills so that an organization can add value at all levels[416].

Humility

Humility is founded upon three powerful pillars[417]. The first pillar is a correct understanding of oneself – including the capacity to view the self in terms of one's highest and best potential as well as the ability to recognize and acknowledge one's imperfections and shortcomings[418]. By clearly understanding oneself, a steward has the ability to assess his or her capabilities and weaknesses and to accommodate them effectively in the leadership role. The second pillar is the ability to correctly assess others, their potential, and their needs[419]. One of the great qualities of a steward is his or her ability to treat others so well that they seek to fulfill their highest potential[420]. The third pillar of humility is the commitment to constantly improve – reflecting an individual's sense of personal responsibility to become a better person[421].

Humility is often accompanied by a fierce resolve to achieve excellence[422]. A steward is motivated by the desire to optimize the ability of others to achieve what is potentially possible[423] and views the obligation to contribute to that opportunity as a personal obligation. Recognizing that greatness is achievable, a steward willingly pursues a plan of action that utilizes the capabilities of others to complement herself or himself. The drive

---

[416] The importance of empowering individuals at all levels is a fundamental quality of high-performance organizations and is described in Beer, M., (2009). *High Commitment High Performance: How to Build a Resilient Organization for Sustained Advantage*. San Francisco, CA: Jossey-Bass.

[417] The research on humility in identifying its three pillars owes a great deal to Owens, B. P. & Hekman, D. R., (2016). "How Does Leader Humility Influence Team Performance? Exploring the Mechanisms of Contagion and Collective Promotion Focus." *Academy of Management Journal*, Vol. 59, Iss. 3, pp. 1086-1111.

[418] *Ibid.*

[419] *Ibid.*

[420] Covey, S. R., (2004), *op. cit.*, p. 98.

[421] Owens, B. P. & Hekman, D. R., (2016), *op. cit.*

[422] Collins, J., (2001), *op. cit.*

[423] Caldwell, C., Hayes, L., and Long, D., (2010), *op. cit.*

to constantly improve and to fulfill what is possible is not motivated by egotism but by the desire to benefit all parties.[424]

> **The drive to constantly improve and to fulfill what is possible is not motivated by egotism but by the desire to benefit all parties.**

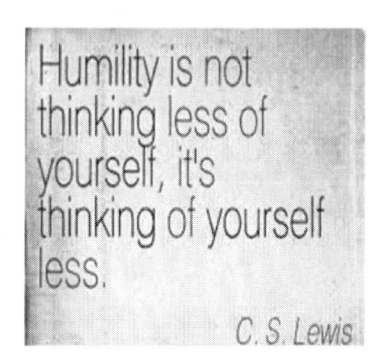

Humility is not thinking less of yourself, it's thinking of yourself less.

C. S. Lewis

When viewed within the context of achieving a noble purpose, a steward's humility guides her or him to pursue that purpose as if it is virtually a personal calling[425]. The steward can actually be surprised that (s)he is in a position to contribute meaningfully to others' lives and is humbled and even in awe of that opportunity[426]. The steward's desire to honor his or her role in contributing to a worthy outcome can leave him or her feeling a sense of deep gratitude, as well as humility, for the opportunity to serve[427].

Love

The role of love in organizational relationships has begun to receive additional attention and has particular applicability to the role of leaders as stewards[428]. Love has been described as the surrender of one's freedom to

---

[424] Caldwell, C., Hayes, L., Karri, R., and Bernal, P., (2008), *op. cit.*

[425] This point about humility and a noble purpose and its implications as a calling is addressed in Anderson, V. & Caldwell, C., (2018). *Humility as Enlightened Leadership*. Hauppage, NY: NOVA Publishing.

[426] *Ibid.*

[427] *Ibid.*

[428] Caldwell, C., (2018), *op. cit.*

others[429] and the gift of oneself[430]. Stewards who choose service to others over their own self-interest willingly give of their efforts to enable others to succeed and to achieve virtuous organizational outcomes[431]. Scott Peck described love as a commitment to the welfare, growth, and wholeness of others[432]. Leaders who demonstrate that love toward those with whom they work have found that authentically caring about others' welfare generates positively deviant extra-role behaviors – including higher commitment, increased creativity, improved quality, and better productivity[433].

Through honoring relationships with others and caring about the welfare of those whom they serve, leaders tap into the best within themselves while bringing out the best in others[434]. Love, like trust, is an emotional skill in which one individual gives willingly of herself or himself in pursuit of another's interests[435]. Love is an affective attribute but it is also based upon a conscious cognitive desire to benefit another, often unconditionally[436]. In his book, *The Art of Loving*, Erich Fromm explained that loving others requires that we put our efforts at risk through caring about another without attempting to control or manipulate their behavior[437].

The ability to love others begins by first loving ourselves and valuing our own personal worth[438]. The steward recognizes her/his own capacity to serve and to help others and has a shared interest in others' welfare and

---

[429] The idea of love as the giving up of one's freedom to another is found in Koestenbaum, P., (2002). *Leadership: The Inner Side of Greatness, A Philosophy for Leaders, New and Revised*. San Francisco, CA: Jossey-Bass.

[430] Robert Greenleaf describes love as the leader's gift of self in Greenleaf, R. K., (1998). *The Power of Servant Leadership*. San Francisco, CA: Berrett-Koehler Publishers.

[431] Block, P., (2013), *op. cit.*

[432] Peck, M. S., (2003). *The Road Less Traveled Timeless Edition: A New Psychology of Love, Traditional Values, and Spiritual Growth*. New York: Touchstone.

[433] Cameron makes this point as a result of extensive research in Cameron, K. S. (2003). "Ethics, Virtuousness, and Constant Change", in N. M. Tichy and A. R. McGill (Eds.), *The Ethical Challenge: How to Lead with Unyielding Integrity*. San Francisco, CA: Jossey-Bass, pp. 185–194.

[434] See Quinn, R. E. (2005). "Moments of Greatness." *Harvard Business Review*, Vol. 83, Iss. 7/8, pp. 74–83.

[435] For a comparison of love and trust, see Caldwell, C., and Dixon, R. D. (2010). "Love, Forgiveness, and Trust: Critical Values of the Modern Leader." *Journal of Business Ethics*, Vol. 93, Iss. 1, pp. 91-101.

[436] Peck, M. S., (2003), *op. cit.*

[437] Fromm, E., (1956). *The Art of Loving*. New York: Harper & Row.

[438] *Ibid.*

success[439]. Stewards receive a great personal satisfaction in knowing that their efforts matter in the lives of others and in their ability to serve their organization and benefit the larger community[440].

Love, like trust, is an emotional skill in which one individual gives willingly of herself or himself in pursuit of another's interests.

As virtuous leaders, stewards willingly accept the responsibility and accountability associated with the mantle of leadership and view service to others as a personal opportunity that fulfills their identity.

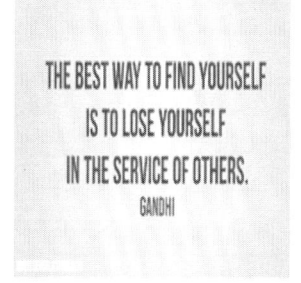

THE BEST WAY TO FIND YOURSELF IS TO LOSE YOURSELF IN THE SERVICE OF OTHERS.
GANDHI

Each of these five virtues is interrelated with the other four and serves to reinforce the steward's commitment to excellence, to service, and to the welfare of others[441]. As virtuous leaders, stewards willingly accept the responsibility and accountability associated with the mantle of leadership[442] and view service to others as a personal opportunity that fulfills their identity[443].

---

[439] This point is made in Okpala, C. O. & Caldwell, C. (2019). "Humility, Forgiveness, and Love: The Heart of Ethical Stewardship." Paper accepted for publication in the *Journal of Values-Based Leadership* in Summer 2019.

[440] Anderson, V. & Caldwell, C., (2018), *op. cit.*

[441] *Ibid.*

[442] The overlap between responsible leadership and virtuous leadership is addressed in Cameron, K., (2011). "Responsible Leadership as Virtuous Leadership." *Journal of Business Ethics*, Vol. 98, pp. 25-35.

[443] Anderson, V. & Caldwell, C., (2018), *op. cit.*

INCORPORATING STEWARDSHIP VIRTUES

Stewardship as a leadership concept has the potential to make a significant difference on organizations, on their members, and on society by effectively utilizing organizational resources to create long-term value[444]. Acquiring the five virtues of leadership not only enables those who lead to be worthy of the trust of others, but also benefits the individuals who strive to obtain those qualities. Those who lead or who wish to lead may benefit by incorporating each of these virtues in their lives. We offer six insights for those who seek to acquire these virtues[445].

Conduct a Regular and Thorough Self-Inventory

A wide variety of resources are available to assist leaders to conduct such an inventory, but the outcome demands a genuine and wholehearted personal commitment. This examination should encompass all aspects of one's life, including a leader's responsibilities in his or her many life roles. This self-assessment is a fundamental building block of humility and a necessary step in changing individual lives[446].

This self-assessment is a fundamental building block of humility and a necessary step in changing individual lives.

---

[444] Caldwell, C., Hayes, L., and Long, D., (2010), *op. cit.*
[445] This list of six insights are found in Okpala, C. O. & Caldwell, C. (2019), *op. cit.*
[446] Anderson, V. & Caldwell, C., (2018), *op. cit.*

Make a Commitment

Once the self-inventory is completed, a commitment is required to make changes in one's personal choices and habits. Individuals undertaking the process of acquiring these five virtues must love themselves enough to recognize that the outcome of changing their lives will be worth the effort[447].

> **Once the self-inventory is completed, a commitment is required to make changes in one's personal choices and habits.**

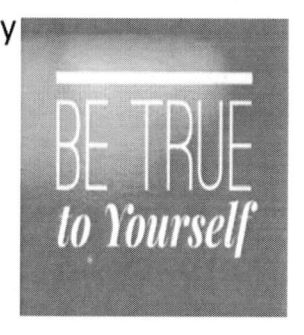

Create a Self-Improvement Partnership

Making a commitment to improve is most effective when that commitment is shared openly with the people who will be affected by the changes. Those who seek to change must be willing to ask others for their support – and for their forgiveness, patience, and feedback during the improvement process[448].

> **Those who seek to change must be willing to ask others for their support – and for their forgiveness, patience, and feedback during the improvement process.**

---

[447] Okpala, C. O. & Caldwell, C., (2019), *op. cit.*

[448] The importance of making a public commitment to changing is suggested by Hansen, M. T., (2018). *Great at Work: How Top Performers Do Less, Work Better, and Achieve More.* New York: Simon & Schuster.

Identify Challenging but Realistic Goals

Dividing your goals into small but challenging pieces and keeping track of one improvement at a time is an important part of achieving success[449]. Setting unrealistic goals generates frustration, discouragement, and disappointment[450]. At the same time, have the integrity to challenge yourself so that what you are seeking to accomplish has real value and substance[451].

Have the integrity to challenge yourself so that what you are seeking to accomplish has real value and substance.

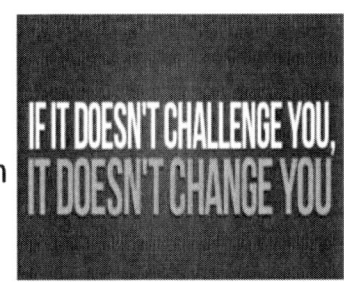

Seek Ongoing Feedback

Commit yourself to creating a process for obtaining feedback about your specific work-related goals but about goals set in other areas in your life. Make your quest for improvement legitimate and involve the people you serve, and care about, to accomplish what matters most to you in your life[452].

Commit yourself to creating a process for obtaining feedback about your specific work-related goals but about goals set in other areas in your life.

---

[449] *Ibid.*
[450] *Ibid.*
[451] Okpala, C. O. & Caldwell, C., (2019), *op. cit.*
[452] *Ibid.*

Celebrate Your Progress

Although you may find that you are not yet where you would someday like to be, give yourself credit along the way for beginning a great journey -- and make this process one of the great successes of your life.

Remember to reward yourself along the way, acknowledge your progress, admit where you need to work harder, and modify what may not seem to work[453]. Throughout the self-improvement process, be good to yourself. Although you may find that you are not yet where you would someday like to be, give yourself credit along the way for beginning a great journey -- and make this process one of the great successes of your life[454].

CONCLUSION

Raising the standard for one's personal performance is far easier than actually achieving that standard. Changing oneself is hard work . . . but it is inevitably worth the price[455]. W. Edwards Deming, universally recognized as "The Father of Quality Improvement," has reminded us that "There is no instant pudding in the improvement process[456]." Becoming a steward demands a commitment to learning that incorporates all four parts of the TRA learning process and requires the ability to acquire insights through each of those four.

---

[453] Hansen, M. T. (2018), *op. cit.*
[454] Okpala, C. O. & Caldwell, C., (2019), *op. cit.*
[455] This insight is emphasized throughout Anderson, V. & Caldwell, C., (2018), *op. cit.*
[456] Deming, W. E., (2000), *Out of the Crisis*. Cambridge, MA: MIT Press.

Changing oneself is hard work . . . but it is inevitably worth the price.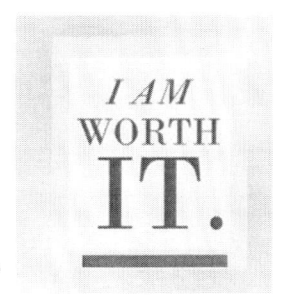

Ultimately, changing one's life by acquiring the five virtues of stewardship is an exciting journey worth pursuing. Becoming a person who exemplifies each of those five virtues is in many ways a lifelong quest . . but it is an effort worth beginning which promises not only the ability to make a significant difference in the lives of others but is a means to fulfill one's own personal potential in becoming the best that one can be. As individuals find their voice and become ethical stewards they also recognize the great satisfaction that can come from also helping others to find their own unique significance and potential as well[457].

REFERENCES

Anderson, V. & Caldwell, C., (2018). *Humility as Enlightened Leadership*. Hauppauge, New York: Nova Science Publishing.

Anderson, L. W. & Krathwohl, D. R., (2000). *A Taxonomy for Learning, Teaching, and Assessing: A Revision of Bloom's Taxonomy of Educational Objectives*. New York: Pearson Publishing.

Beer, M., (2009). *High Commitment High Performance: How to Build a Resilient Organization for Sustained Advantage*. San Francisco, CA: Jossey-Bass.

Block, P., (2013). *Stewardship: Choosing Service Over Self-Interest*. San Francisco, CA: Jossey-Bass.

---

[457] Covey, S. R., (2004), *op. cit.*

Caldwell, C., (2018). *Leadership, Ethics, and Trust*. Newcastle upon Tyne, UK: Cambridge Scholars Publishing.

Caldwell, C. & Anderson, V., (2017). *Competitive Advantage: Strategies, Management, and Performance*. Hauppauge, NY: Nova Science Publishers.

Caldwell, C., Atwijuka, S. & Oklpala, C. O., (2018). "Compassionate Leadership in an Arms-Length World." Paper accepted for publication in the *Journal of Business Administration and Management*.

Caldwell, C., Hayes, L., and Long, D., (2010). "Leadership, Trustworthiness, and Ethical Stewardship." *Journal of Business Ethics*, Vol. 96, Iss. 4, pp. 497-512.

Caldwell, C., and Dixon, R. D. (2010). "Love, Forgiveness, and Trust: Critical Values of the Modern Leader." *Journal of Business Ethics*, Vol. 93, Iss. 1, pp. 91-101.

Caldwell, C., Hayes, L., Karri, R., and Bernal, P., (2008). "Ethical Stewardship: The Role of Leadership Behavior and Perceived Trustworthiness." *Journal of Business Ethics*, Vol. 78, Iss. 1/2, pp. 153-164.

Caldwell, C., Hayes, L., Karri, R., and Bernal, P., (2008), *op. cit.* and Mezirow, J., (1996). "Toward a Learning Theory of Adult Literacy." *Adult Basic Education*, Vol. 6, No. 3, pp. 115-126.

Cameron, K., (2011). "Responsible Leadership as Virtuous Leadership." *Journal of Business Ethics*, Vol. 98, pp. 25-35.

Cameron, K. S. (2003). "Ethics, Virtuousness, and Constant Change", in N. M. Tichy and A. R. McGill (Eds.), *The Ethical Challenge: How to Lead with Unyielding Integrity*. San Francisco, CA: Jossey-Bass, pp. 185–194.

Christensen, C. M., (2016). *The Innovator's Dilemma: When New Technologies Cause Great Firms to Fail*. Boston, MA: Harvard Business Review Press.

Collins, J., (2001). *Good to Great: Why Some Companies Make the Leap . . . . And Others Don't*. New York: HarperCollins.

Covey, S. R., (2004). The 8th Habit: From Effectiveness to Greatness. New York: Free Press and in Kouzes, J. M. & Posner, B. Z., (2017). *The*

Leadership Challenge: How to Make Extraordinary Things Happen in Organizations (6th ed.). San Francisco, CA: Jossey-Bass.

DePree, M., (2004). *Leadership is an Art*. New York: Crown Publishing.

Fink, A. K., & Fink, L. D. (2009). Lessons we Learn from the Voices of Experience. *New Directions for Teaching & Learning,* Vol. 119, pp. 105-113.

Fink, L. D., (2003). *Creating Significant Learning Experiences: An Integrated Approach for Designing College Courses*. San Francisco, CA: Jossey-Bass.

Fishbein, M. & Ajzen, I., (2015). *Predicting and Changing Behavior: The Reasoned Action Approach*. New York: Psychology Press.

Gilligan, C., (2016). *In a Different Voice: Psychological Theory and Women's Development*. Boston, MA: Harvard University Press.

Glasper, K. & Caldwell, C., (2016). "Teaching Through 'Transforming Learning,' an Integrative Model for Business and Public Administration Education." *Business and Management Research,* Vol. 5, No. 1, pp. 19-28 and available online at http://www.sciedupress.com/journal/index.php/bmr/article/view/9088/5495.

Graham, P., (2003). *Mary Parker Follett: Prophet of Management*. Washington, D.C.: Beard Books.

Greenleaf, R. K. & Spears, L. C., (2002). *Servant Leadership: A Journey Into Legitimate Power and Greatness 25th Anniversary Edition*. Mahwah, NJ: Paulist Press.

Greenleaf, R. K., (1998). *The Power of Servant Leadership*. San Francisco, CA: Berrett-Koehler Publishers.

Hansen, M. T., (2018). *Great at Work: How Top Performers Do Less, Work Better, and Achieve More*. New York: Simon & Schuster.

Hernandez, M., (2012). "Toward an Understanding of the Psychology of Stewardship." *Academy of Management Review*, Vol. 37, Iss. 2, pp. 172-193.

Koestenbaum, P., (2002). *Leadership: The Inner Side of Greatness, A Philosophy for Leaders, New and Revised*. San Francisco, CA: Jossey-Bass.

Kohlberg, L., (1981), *The Philosophy of Moral Development: Moral Stages and the Idea of Justice*. New York: Harper & Row.

Lennick, D. & Kiel, F., (2015). *Moral Intelligence 2.0: Enhancing Business Performance and Leadership Success in Turbulent Times*. Upper Saddle River, NJ: FT Press.

Okpala, C. O. & Caldwell, C. (2019). "Humility, Forgiveness, and Love: The Heart of Ethical Stewardship." Paper accepted for publication in the *Journal of Values-Based Leadership* in Summer 2019.

Owens, B. P. & Hekman, D. R., (2016). "How Does Leader Humility Influence Team Performance? Exploring the Mechanisms of Contagion and Collective Promotion Focus." *Academy of Management Journal*, Vol. 59, Iss. 3, pp. 1086-1111.

Peck, M. S., (2003). *The Road Less Traveled Timeless Edition: A New Psychology of Love, Traditional Values, and Spiritual Growth*. New York: Touchstone.

Price, Q., (2015). *7 Habits of Highly Resilient People: How to Make the Most of Loss, Change and Setbacks*. Seattle, WA: CreateSpace Independent Publishing.

Quinn, R. E. (2005). "Moments of Greatness." *Harvard Business Review*, Vol. 83, Iss. 7/8, pp. 74–83.

Senge, P. M., (2006). *The Fifth Discipline: The Art & Practice of the Learning Organization*. New York: Random House.

Schein, E. H. & Schein, P., (2016). *Organizational Culture and Leadership* (4th ed.). San Francisco, CA: Jossey-Bass.

Schopenhauer, A., (2016). *The Wisdom of Life*. Seattle, WA: Create Space Independent Publishing.

Simon, H. A., (1997). *Administrative Behavior* (4th ed.). New York: Free Press.

Chapter 11

THE VIRTUOUS REWARD – FINDING YOUR VOICE AND THE MORAL DUTY

In his lifelong pursuit of excellence, Stephen R. Covey, sought to share with others principles of truth that can enable them to be more personally successful, to increase their capacity to serve others, and to benefit the world around them. Covey's *7 Habits of Highly Effective People* has sold more than 25 million copies worldwide, has been translated into 38 different languages, and its audio book has sold more than a million copies. Significantly, Covey has written a sequel to his best-selling book that he developed in response to the demands of a changing world where being "effective" is no longer good enough. Covey's sequel, *The 8th Habit: From Effectiveness to Greatness*, provides those who seek to be optimally successful to "find your voice, and then inspire others to find theirs."

Covey's wisdom about the importance of self-discovery, the need to become greater than you have ever been, and the obligation to help others to then become their best is at the heart of ethical stewardship and empowers others to not only become influential servant leaders but to optimize their ability to add value in the world. The purposes of this chapter are to address the importance of "finding your voice" as a virtuous personal achievement and to then honor the moral obligation to discover their own unique significance and potential. The chapter begins with a review of the importance of adding value to society – incorporating both Jim Collins' "Hedgehog Concept" and Covey's insights about finding one's voice. After clarifying why finding our own voice is so critical to being a virtuous leader, we then address why helping others to also achieve their best version of themselves is a moral imperative of leaders as well. We conclude the chapter with brief comments about the importance of leaders becoming not only responsible leaders but also virtuous stewards in their service to others.

" FIND YOUR VOICE *and* **INSPIRE OTHERS TO FIND THEIRS. "** - *Stephen Covey*

Covey's wisdom about the importance of self-discovery, the need to become greater than you have ever been, and the obligation to help others to then become their best is at the heart of ethical stewardship and empowers others to not only become influential servant leaders but to optimize their ability to add value in the world.

ADDING VALUE AS A MORAL IMPERATIVE

Whether we are engaged in life in a commercial business, a non-profit organization, or as independent individuals each one of us shares the obligation to add value to others and to the world in which we live. The universal axiom is that "Service is the rent we pay for living in the world[458]." Moral intelligence encompasses 1) doing no harm, 2) adding value in the short term, and 3) adding value in the long term[459]. As employees or as members of a household, our contribution to others is often perceived to be the measure of our individual worth or contribution of value – and how we add value differentiates us in the eyes of others.

---

[458] This statement has been attributed to many individuals. See, for example, Edelman, M. W., (1993). *The Measure of Our Success: A Letter to My Children and Yours*. New York: Harper Perennial.

[459] The values and obligations of moral intelligence are identified in Lennick, D. & Kiel, F., (2016). *Moral Intelligence 2.0: Enhancing Business Performance and Leadership Success in Turbulent Times*. Boston, MA: Pearson Education.

Moral intelligence encompasses 1) doing no harm, 2) adding value in the short term, and 3) adding value in the long term

The Hedgehog Concept

Our ability to add value in business is the focus of what business expert, Jim Collins, labeled "The Hedgehog Concept[460]." Citing the ancient Greek parable about the fox and the hedgehog, Collins explained that "the fox knows many things but the hedgehog knows one big thing[461]." Relating the metaphor to business success, Collins noted that a firm needed to focus on the overlap of three critical insights about its focus[462].

1. *What it is Deeply Passionate about.* Collins explained that individuals and companies must have a deep personal commitment to what it does. This emotional dedication to a focused interest enables individuals to persist and endure over time in the pursuit of an important objective.

2. *What it can Accomplish at a World Class Level.* To be successful, one must understand what they are able to do at a level that adds value that cannot be duplicated easily by others. This quality requires the capacity to demonstrate refined excellence.

---

[460] Collins cited this concept in his award-winning book, Good to Great. See Collins, J., (2001). *Good to Great: Why Some Companies Make the Leap . . . And Others Don't.* New York: HarperCollins.

[461] *Ibid.*

[462] *Ibid.*

3. *What Drives Your Economic Engine.* Collins emphasized that this quality equated to the world being willing to pay for the service or product that you provide in an amount that exceeds your costs.

Figure 1 provides a visual portrayal of the three overlapping circles that form this Hedgehog Concept[463]."

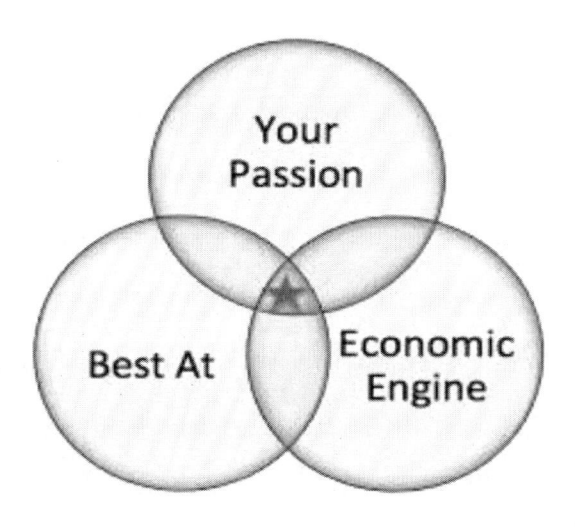

Your Passion

Best At

Economic Engine

Figure 1. Collins' Hedgehog Concept.

The competency to be excellent, the ability to recognize what others value, and the realization of what one is passionate about doing combine to identify where an individual or organization can make the greatest contribution to the world.

The competency to be excellent, the ability to recognize what others value, and the realization of what one is passionate about doing combine to

---

[463] *Ibid.*

identify where an individual or organization can make the greatest contribution to the world, according to Collins[464].

Four Intelligences

Stephen R. Covey suggested that each person possess four "intelligences" which he used as the basis for determining how to assess one's unique significance[465]. These four intelligences interrelate and provide the basis for each person's capacity to add value. Covey labeled these intelligences as follows.

- *IQ or Mental Intelligence* – An IQ is a standardized measure of mental intelligence compared to that of other people. IQ is basically cognitive or academic intelligence that measures one's knowledge associated with a well-defined goal and structure.

An IQ is a standardized measure of mental intelligence compared to that of other people. IQ is basically cognitive or academic intelligence that measures one's knowledge associated with a well-defined goal and structure.

- *PQ of Physical Intelligence* – PQ is defined as the intelligence related to the natural aspects of the functions of your body associated with such things as physical fitness, endurance, and overall physical health. PQ relates to our ability to maintain and develop physical skills.

---

[464] *Ibid.*
[465] Covey, S. R., (2004). *The 8th Habit: From Effectiveness to Greatness*. New York: Free Press.

PQ is defined as the intelligence related to the natural aspects of the functions of your body associated with such things as physical fitness, endurance, and overall physical health. PQ relates to our ability to maintain and develop physical skills.

- *EQ or Emotional Intelligence* – The EQ is our ability to relate to others interpersonally at the emotional level, to show empathy, and compassion, and to act appropriately in collaborative relationships. EQ includes our self-knowledge, self-awareness, social sensitivity, and our ability to communicate successfully with others from our heart.

The EQ is our ability to relate to others interpersonally at the emotional level, to show empathy, and compassion, and to act appropriately in collaborative relationships. EQ includes our self-knowledge, self-awareness, social sensitivity, and our ability to communicate successfully with others from our heart.

- *SQ or Spiritual Intelligence* – One's SQ relates to one's values and the capacity to be driven by one's conscience and refers to the ability to find meaning and to connect with the infinite as a source of directing personal choices.

One's SQ relates to one's values and the capacity to be driven by one's conscience and refers to the ability to find meaning and to connect with the infinite as a source of directing personal choices.

Figure 2 shows the relationship of these four intelligences and identifies the role of one's conscience in directing individual choices.

Figure 2. Covey's Four Intelligences.

Each of these four intelligences interacts with the other three and plays an important role in contributing to decisions about what we consider to be important, what we are capable of accomplishing, and what matters most in our individual lives[466]. The ability to develop and refine each of the four

---

[466] *Ibid.*

intelligences is also a factor in determining the capacity to add value. Each of these four intelligences also plays an important role in framing an individual's personal identity and that which is central, enduring, and distinctive in a person's life[467]. Developing and enhancing each of these four intelligences requires personal vision, a recognition of one's duties and responsibilities, one's capacity for faith in action, and one's individual discipline and character[468].

Each of these four intelligences also plays an important role in framing an individual's personal identity and that which is central, enduring, and distinctive in a person's life.

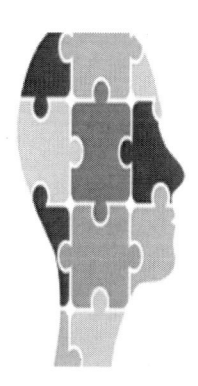

Adapting the Hedgehog Concept to the four intelligences, Covey suggested that, like Collins' three capacities, the four intelligences are useful as a powerful tool in understanding more about how a person should focus his or her efforts in life choices. Understanding each of these four intelligences and incorporating them fully into one's life enables a person to maintain a sense of balance, a life of individual fulfillment, increased self-awareness, and previously unrealized personal achievement.

Cognitive intelligence provides the conceptual understanding and knowledge necessary to solve a problem or develop an idea. However, that knowledge must also be properly applied. What is known must be contextually appropriate for the situation requiring a response. Subtle nuances of understanding are required in differentiating between what is

---

[467] This point is emphasized in Caldwell, C. (2009). "Identity, Self-Deception, and Self-Awareness: Ethical Implications for Leaders and Organizations." *Journal of Business Ethics*, Vol. 90, Supp. 3, pp. 393-406.
[468] Covey, S. R., (2004), *op. cit.*

most important and that which matters far less – particularly by identifying root causes rather than the symptoms associated with a problem to be resolved. Cognitive competence is necessary but not sufficient to earn the personal credibility of others.

Subtle nuances of understanding are required in differentiating between what is most important and that which matters far less – particularly by identifying root causes rather than the symptoms associated with a problem to be resolved.

Fitness and good health often make the difference when it is necessary to engage in a complex assignment that may take months, years, or even decades to accomplish. The capacity to perform is essential to earning others' trust.

Physical capabilities, dexterity, strength, endurance, speed, and coordination of actions are also required to accomplish many objectives. Many tasks require skills that take extensive preparation and practice. The ability to concentrate one's efforts, to focus on a problem, and the tenacity to follow-through until a task is done often requires both a mental ability and a matching set of physical skills that complement the desire to achieve a valued result. Fitness and good health often make the difference when it is necessary to engage in a complex assignment that may take months, years, or even decades to accomplish. The capacity to perform is essential to earning others' trust.

Emotional intelligence and genuine love are necessary elements that are required to be able to accomplish many important achievements. Self-awareness, self-discipline, empathy, self-mastery, and an understanding of what unique situations require demand that the person responding understands the situation and context and is willing to help others to accomplish an important outcome. A key element of emotional intelligence in creating high trust is an authentic concern for others and their needs.

Self-awareness, self-discipline, empathy, self-mastery, and an understanding of what unique situations require demand that the person responding understands the situation and context and is willing to help others to accomplish an important outcome.

Added to that which people love to do, what they do well, and what others believe adds value, the Spiritual Intelligence affirms what an individual knows (s)he should do – in addition to what (s)he is capable of doing.

Covey suggested that the introduction of the fourth circle associated with Spiritual Intelligence, or conscience, can provide moral clarity. Added to that which people love to do, what they do well, and what others believe adds value, the Spiritual Intelligence affirms what an individual knows (s)he should do – in addition to what (s)he is capable of doing.

Figure 3. Covey's Concept of Voice.

Covey called the overlapping of these four intelligences one's "Voice" or unique significance. Figure 3 is a representation of Covey's model of the concept of Voice or unique significance.

Finding one's voice opens up a world of self-discovery that enables a person to become a better person than they previously had imagined that they had the ability to become. One's voice enables a person to recognize and fulfill their unique capabilities and to contribute to the lives of others, as well as achieving personal fulfillment.

It is in expressing one's voice by fully incorporating all four intelligences that an individual becomes a force that draws him or her to their next level of self-awareness and achievement. People who choose not to or who are unable to find their voice often wander aimlessly and feel frustrated without realizing what they are missing in their lives. Finding one's voice opens up a world of self-discovery that enables a person to become a better person than they previously had imagined that they had the ability to become. One's voice enables a person to recognize and fulfill their unique capabilities and to contribute to the lives of others, as well as achieving personal fulfillment.

FINDING YOUR VOICE AND THE LEADER'S CHALLENGE

Covey defined leadership as treating others so well that they come to recognize their own potential greatness and strive to achieve it[469]. Great leaders who adopt a stewardship responsibility toward others recognize that leadership is both transformational and transformative. Transformational leaders fully acknowledge the obligation of leaders to benefit both the organization and the individuals within it[470]. They understand that the obligation owed to employees is far more than a transactional, quid pro quo exchange of money for services provided. Transformative leaders seek to honor a broad range of ethical standards that seek the highest and best organizational and individual growth and achievement while honoring commitments made and relationships developed[471].

The challenge for leaders as organizational stewards is to develop personal relationships that enable them to understand the strengths of their colleagues as well as the areas in which others need to improve. Leaders who reach out to others, who listen to their concerns and priorities, help the to grow and to learn, and who empower them to develop their skills are uncommon in today's arms-length world[472]. Stewards honor the obligation of servant leadership to be "a servant and a debtor" to others as they seek to help them to accomplish their personal goals[473].

---

[469] *Ibid*, p. 98.
[470] Transformational leadership is explained and clarified in Burns, J. M., (2010). Leaders.
[471] For a review of transformative leadership and its responsibilities toward others, see Caldwell, C., Dixon, R. D., Floyd, L., Chaudoin, J., Post., J., and Cheokas, G. (2012). "Transformative Leadership: Achieving Unparalleled Excellence." *Journal of Business Ethics*, Vol 109, Iss. 2, pp. 175-187 and Ali Habi Al, H., Sayed, R. T., and Caldwell, C., (2019). "Transformative Ethics and Moving Toward 'Greatness.' – Problems and Realities." Paper accepted for publication in the *Journal of Values-Based Leadership* in March 2019.
[472] See Caldwell, C., Atwijuka, S. & Okpala, C. O., (2018)"Compassionate Leadership in an Arms-Length World." Working paper currently under review in the *International Journal of Business and Management*.
[473] See DePree, M., (2004). *Leadership is an Art*. New York: Crown Publishing.

Leaders who reach out to others, who listen to their concerns and priorities, help the to grow and to learn, and who empower them to develop their skills are uncommon in today's arms-length world.

Dare to live an

uncommon Life

Moral leadership also includes the obligation to develop within others the capacity to constantly learn and to develop a thorough understanding of the needs of customers, the keys to organizational value creation, and the means by which organizations establish a competitive advantage,

Moral leadership also includes the obligation to develop within others the capacity to constantly learn and to develop a thorough understanding of the needs of customers, the keys to organizational value creation, and the means by which organizations establish a competitive advantage[474]. The obligation of leaders is to ensure that an organization is competent and that its employees have the resources essential to achieve the goals that need to be accomplished. To achieve that objective, great leaders have the obligation to create organizational systems and processes that reinforce values and that enable team members to contribute to the organization's successes[475]. As Covey has explained, the universal mission of organizations is to achieve its highest and best potential in adding value to society by creating the

---

[474] See Pfeffer, J., (1998). *The Human Equation. Building Profits by Putting People First.* Boston, MA: Harvard Business Review Press and Beer, M., (2009). *High Commitment High Performance: How to Build a Resilient Organization for Sustained Advantage.* San Francisco, CA: Jossey- Bass.

[475] *Ibid.*

mechanisms that promote personal development as well as optimizing long-term value creation[476].

In identifying the obligations of leaders, scholars have acknowledged that leaders' responsibilities encompass far more than simply earning profit for owners and shareholders[477]. Organizational leaders have the opportunity to rise to the level of virtuous stewards as they strive to optimize the wealth and value that they create long-term for all of their stakeholders[478]. In identifying the moral responsibility of leaders, the obligation to achieve that which best serves society and other stakeholders by generating the greatest long-term value is not only viewed as a stewardship position but as the desired objective of what has been called "The Virtuous Continuum[479]." That continuum, shown as Figure 4, identifies the distinction between choices that range from the Immoral and Amoral to the Moral and Virtuous[480].

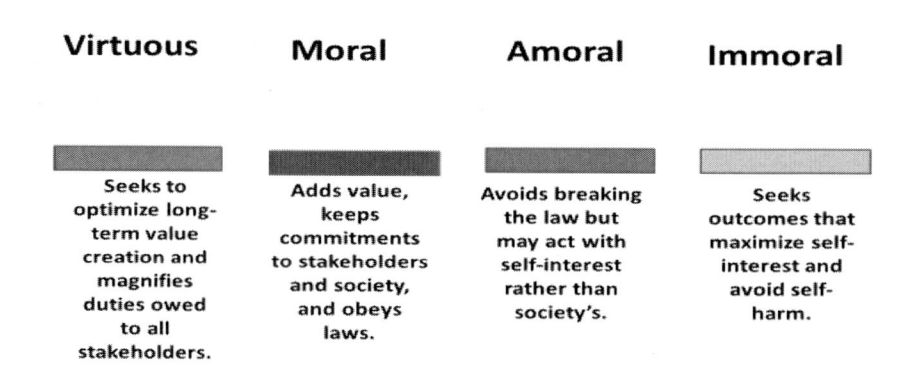

Figure 4. The Virtuous Continuum.

As leaders strive to honor the virtuous obligations articulated on this continuum, they function as ethical stewards, empower others to find their

---

[476] Covey, S. R>, (2004), *op. cit.*, p. 99.

[477] This classic point is the theme of Solomon, R. C., (1993). *Ethics and Excellence: Cooperation and Integrity in Business.* Oxford, UK: Oxford University Press.

[478] This point is emphasized in Caldwell, C., Hasan, Z., and Smith, S. (2015). "Virtuous Leadership: Insights for the 21st Century." *Journal of Management Development.* Vol. 34, Iss. 9, pp. 1181-1200.

[479] *Ibid.*

[480] *Ibid.*

voice, and enable their organizations to optimize long-term wealth creation[481].

CONCLUSION

The University of Michigan's Kim Cameron has emphasized that leaders have the obligation to be responsible and accountable in serving their organizations, honoring duties to society, and creating wealth and adding value[482]. Being responsible addresses the obligation to be both efficient and effective – but Cameron has also suggested that responsible leaders also have the obligation to be virtuous[483].

> The University of Michigan's Kim Cameron has emphasized that leaders have the obligation to be responsible and accountable in serving their organizations, honoring duties to society, and creating wealth and adding value.

RESPONSIBLE LEADERSHIP

That which is virtuous promotes a higher standard than that which is merely moral and beneficial. Cameron suggests that virtuous leadership reflects the highest in moral excellence[484]. Virtuousness promotes that which is flourishing, and incorporates humanity's very best qualities[485].

---

[481] Caldwell, C., Hayes, L., and Long, D., (2010). "Leadership, Trustworthiness, and Ethical Stewardship." *Journal of Business Ethics*, Vol. 96, Iss. 4, pp. 497-512.

[482] Cameron, K., (2011). "Responsible Leadership as Virtuous Leadership." *Journal of Business Ethics*, Vol. 98, pp. 25-35.

[483] *Ibid.*

[484] *Ibid.*

[485] *Ibid.*

Virtuousness in leaders, Cameron reminds us, rises above that which is merely accountable and, though it is desirable, is also rare[486]. Despite the fact that the pursuit of that which is virtuous is uncommon, leaders and organizations that pursue virtuousness are worthy of emulation. Such leaders honor not only their obligation to create value for society, but they serve those with whom they work and enable their colleagues to excel and to become the best possible versions of themselves.

Virtuousness in leaders, Cameron reminds us, rises above that which is merely accountable and, though it is desirable, is also rare.

Leaders who adopt this virtuous commitment become ethical stewards who earn the trust, commitment, and followership that enables organizations to compete successfully while simultaneously honoring their moral obligation to others.

Leaders who adopt this virtuous commitment become ethical stewards who earn the trust, commitment, and followership that enables organizations to compete successfully while simultaneously honoring their moral obligation to others. Such leaders have adopted the mantra of the 8th habit

---

[486] *Ibid*, p. 25.

and have both found their voice and assisted others with whom they work to find their voices as well[487].

REFERENCES

Ali Habi Al, H., Sayed, R. T., and Caldwell, C., (2019). "Transformative Ethics and Moving Toward 'Greatness.' – Problems and Realities." Paper accepted for publication in the *Journal of Values-Based Leadership* in March 2019.

Caldwell, C., Atwijuka, S. & Okpala, C. O., (2018) "Compassionate Leadership in an Arms-Length World." Working paper currently under review in the *International Journal of Business and Management*.

Caldwell, C., Hasan, Z., and Smith, S. (2015). "Virtuous Leadership: Insights for the 21st Century." *Journal of Management Development*. Vol. 34, Iss. 9, pp. 1181-1200.

Caldwell, C., Dixon, R. D., Floyd, L., Chaudoin, J., Post., J., and Cheokas, G. (2012). "Transformative Leadership: Achieving Unparalleled Excellence." *Journal of Business Ethics*, Vol 109, Iss. 2, pp. 175-187

Caldwell, C., Hayes, L., and Long, D., (2010). "Leadership, Trustworthiness, and Ethical Stewardship." *Journal of Business Ethics*, Vol. 96, Iss. 4, pp. 497-512.

Caldwell, C. (2009). "Identity, Self-Deception, and Self-Awareness: Ethical Implications for Leaders and Organizations." *Journal of Business Ethics*, Vol. 90, Supp. 3, pp. 393-406.

Cameron, K., (2011). "Responsible Leadership as Virtuous Leadership." *Journal of Business Ethics*, Vol. 98, pp. 25-35.

Collins, J., (2001). *Good to Great: Why Some Companies Make the Leap . . . and Others Don't*. New York: HarperCollins.

Covey, S. R., (2004). *The 8th Habit: From Effectiveness to Greatness*. New York: Free Press.

DePree, M., (2004). *Leadership is an Art*. New York: Crown Publishing.

---

[487] Covey, S. R., (2004), *op. cit.*

Edelman, M. W., (1993). *The Measure of Our Success: A Letter to My Children and Yours*. New York: Harper Perennial.

Lennick, D. & Kiel, F., (2016). *Moral Intelligence 2.0: Enhancing Business Performance and Leadership Success in Turbulent Times*. Boston, MA: Pearson Education.

Pfeffer, J., (1998). The Human Equation. Building Profits by Putting People First. Boston, MA: *Harvard Business Review* Press and Beer, M., (2009). *High Commitment High Performance: How to Build a Resilient Organization for Sustained Advantage*. San Francisco, CA: Jossey-Bass.

Solomon, R. C., (1993*). Ethics and Excellence: Cooperation and Integrity in Business*. Oxford, UK: Oxford University Press.

ABOUT THE AUTHORS

Cam Caldwell, PhD

Business Professor
University of Illinois Springfield, Springfield, Illinois, US

Dr. Cam Caldwell received his PhD in Human Resources and Organization Behavior from Washington State University where he was a Thomas S. Foley Graduate Fellow. He holds the Senior Professional and Global Professional in Human Resources professional certifications. Prior to earning his PhD, he worked as a Human Resource Director, City Manager, and Management Consultant for more than twenty years. This is his seventh book and he has published many papers about a variety of management and leadership topics.

Verl Anderson, PhD

Business Professor
Dixie State University, St George, Utah, US
Email: verl@dixie.edu

Dr. Verl Anderson obtained his doctorate degree in Business Administration from Arizona State University. He is currently a professor in

Management and International Business at Dixie State University, St George, Utah. He has taught university courses as a visiting professor in New Zealand and four universities in China. He has published 34 articles in the past two years on leadership, ethics, China culture, kindness, strategic management, and social responsibility. His research interests include China culture and international cultures. He has traveled extensively, and annually takes groups on cultural/educational tours to China and New Zealand.

INDEX

Related Nova Publications

A COMPREHENSIVE INVESTIGATION ON EXECUTIVE-EMPLOYEE PAY GAP OF CHINESE ENTERPRISES: ANTECEDENTS AND CONSEQUENCES

AUTHOR: Changzheng Zhang

SERIES: Business Issues, Competition and Entrepreneurship

BOOK DESCRIPTION: The executive-employee compensation gap, a newly focused dimension of the executive compensation packages by the previous literature, has been given a great deal of attention because of the growing inequality in the compensation practices within the firms over the past two decades in China.

HARDCOVER ISBN: 978-1-53612-813-0
RETAIL PRICE: $270

BUSINESS TRENDS IN THE 21ST CENTURY: REGULATIONS AND LEGISLATION

AUTHOR: Cruz Omar Clemente Escamilla

SERIES: Business Issues, Competition and Entrepreneurship

BOOK DESCRIPTION: This book opens with an examination of the economic circumstances of veteran-owned business. It provides a brief overview of veterans' employment experiences, comparing unemployment and labor force participation rates for veterans, veterans who have left the military since September 2001 and nonveterans.

HARDCOVER ISBN: 978-1-53614-260-0
RETAIL PRICE: $160

To see complete list of Nova publications, please visit our website at www.novapublishers.com